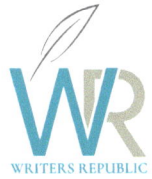

WRITERS REPUBLIC

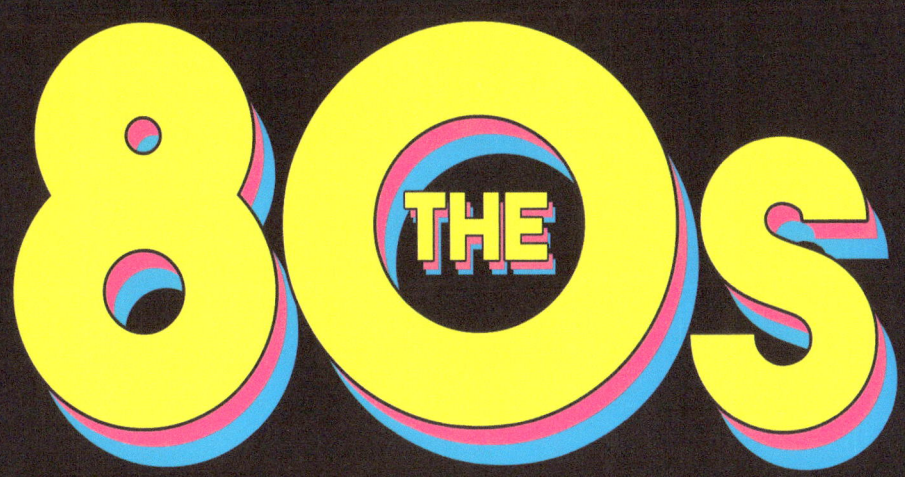

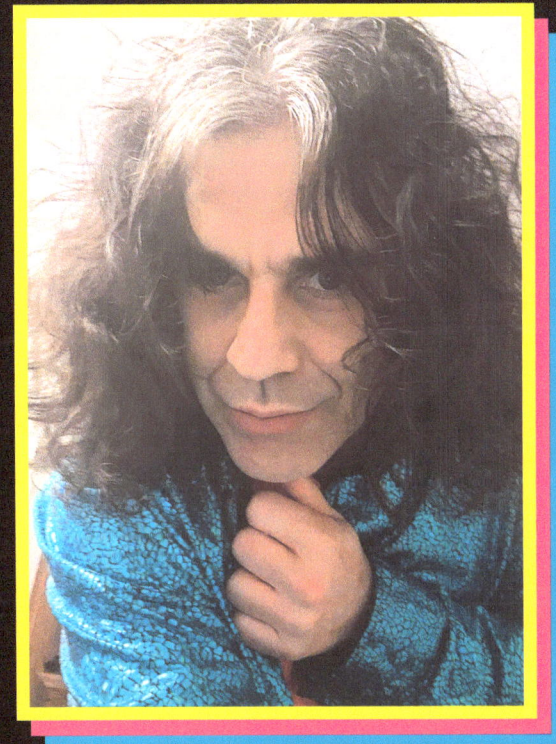

WHAT A DECADE

DONALD G. ENNIS

WRITERS REPUBLIC L.L.C.
515 Summit Ave. Unit R1
Union City, NJ 07087, USA

Website: *www.writersrepublic.com*
Hotline: *1-877-656-6838*
Email: *info@writersrepublic.com*

Ordering Information:
Quantity sales. Special discounts are available on quantity purchases by corporations, associations, and others. For details, contact the publisher at the address above.

Library of Congress Control Number:	2023942830	
ISBN-13:	979-8-89100-066-7	[Paperback Edition]
	979-8-89100-067-4	[Hardback Edition]
	979-8-89100-069-8	[Digital Edition]

Rev. date: 06/21/2023

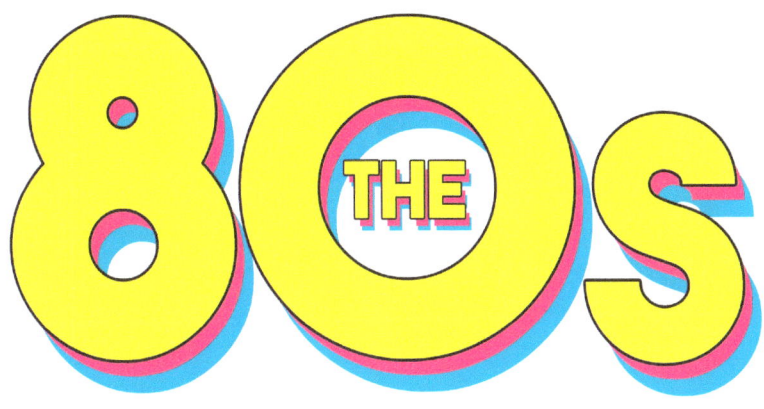

THE 80s

WHAT A DECADE

DONALD G. ENNIS

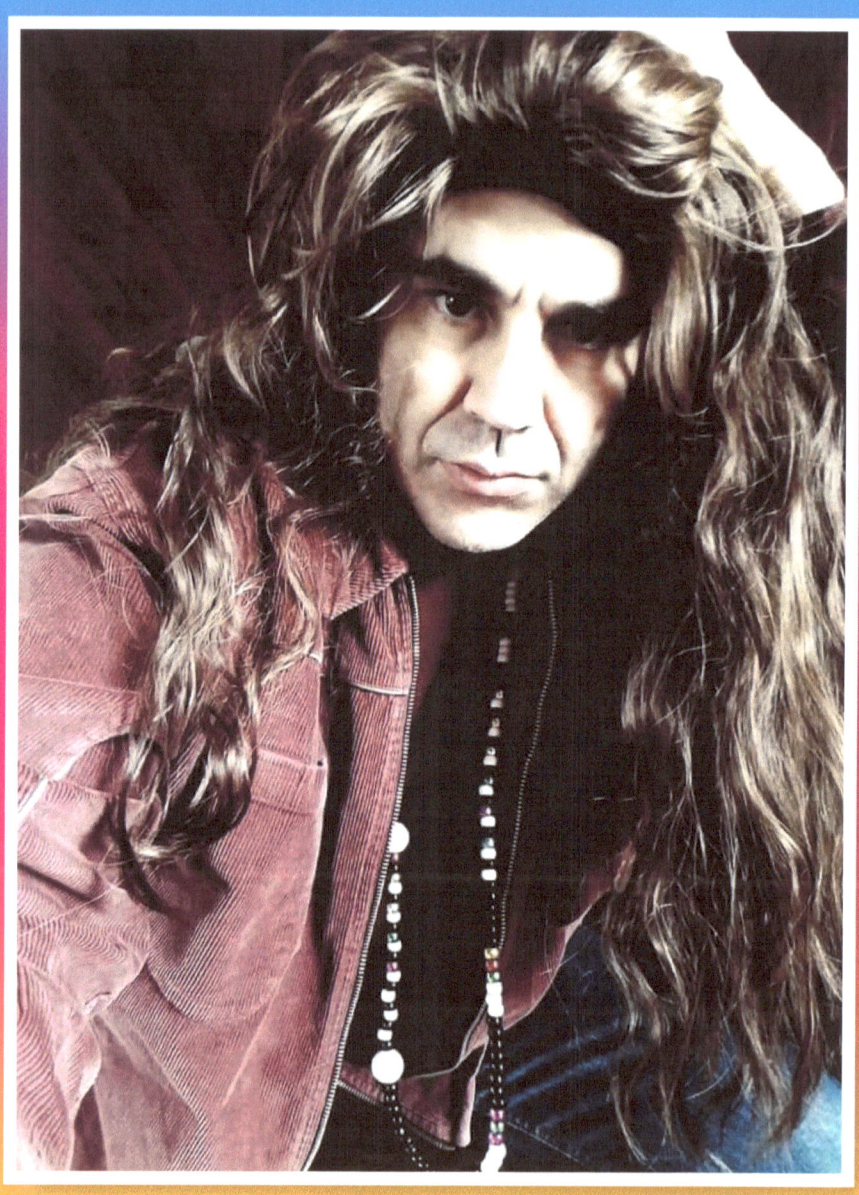

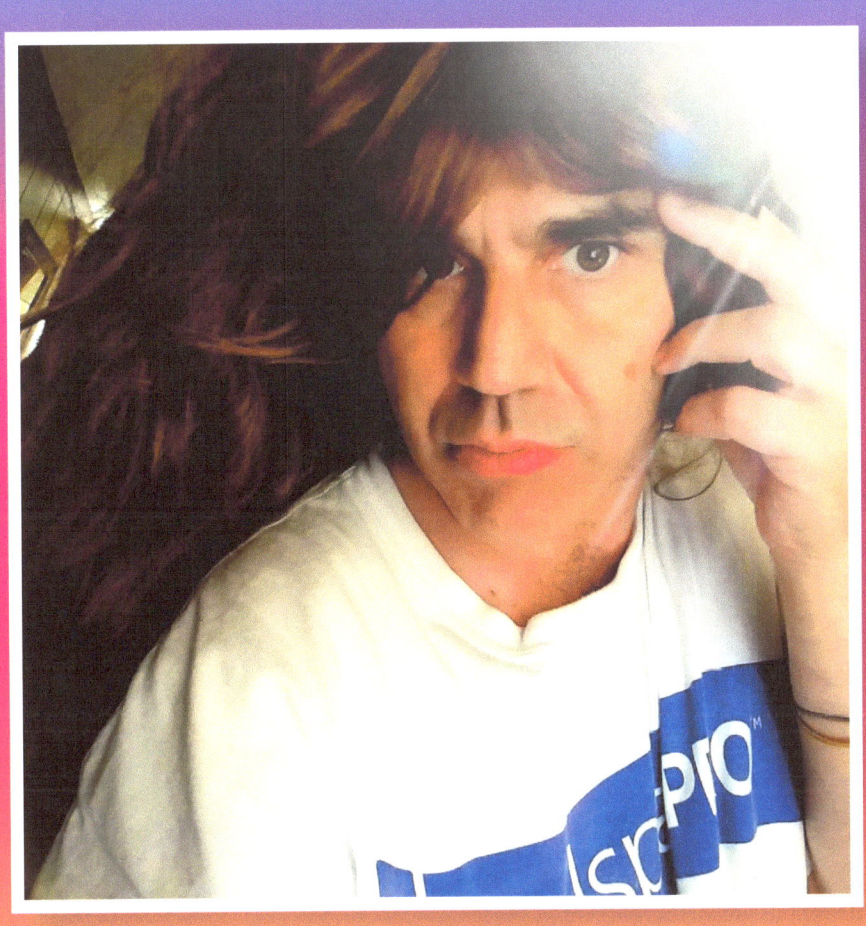

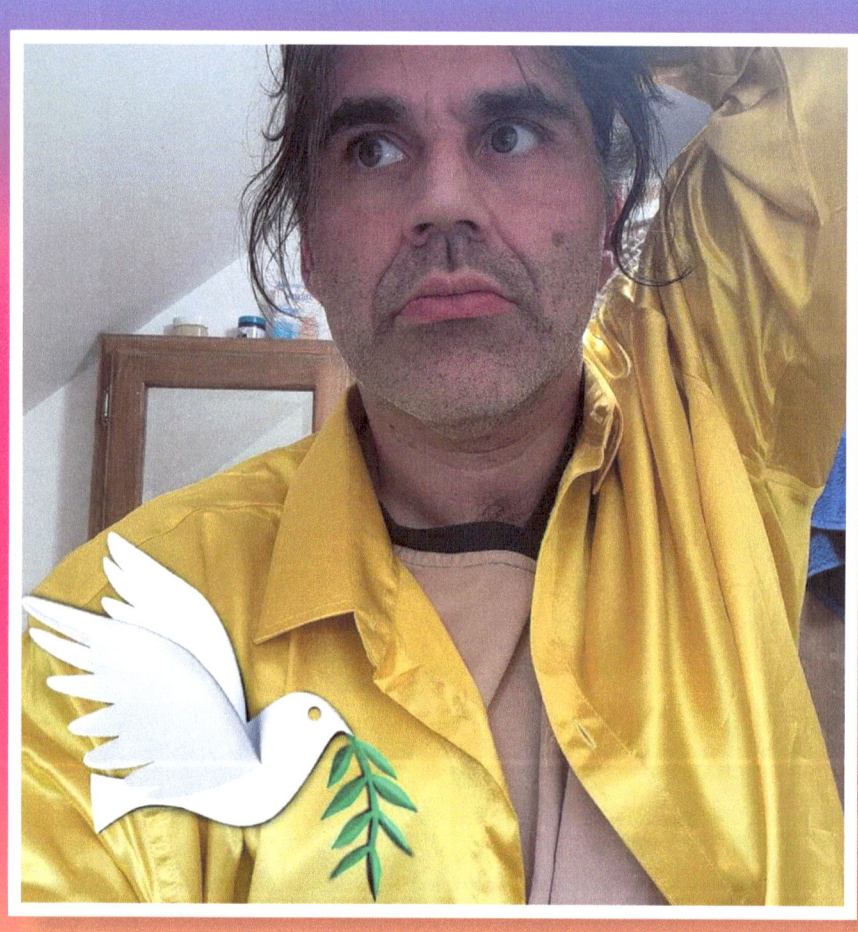

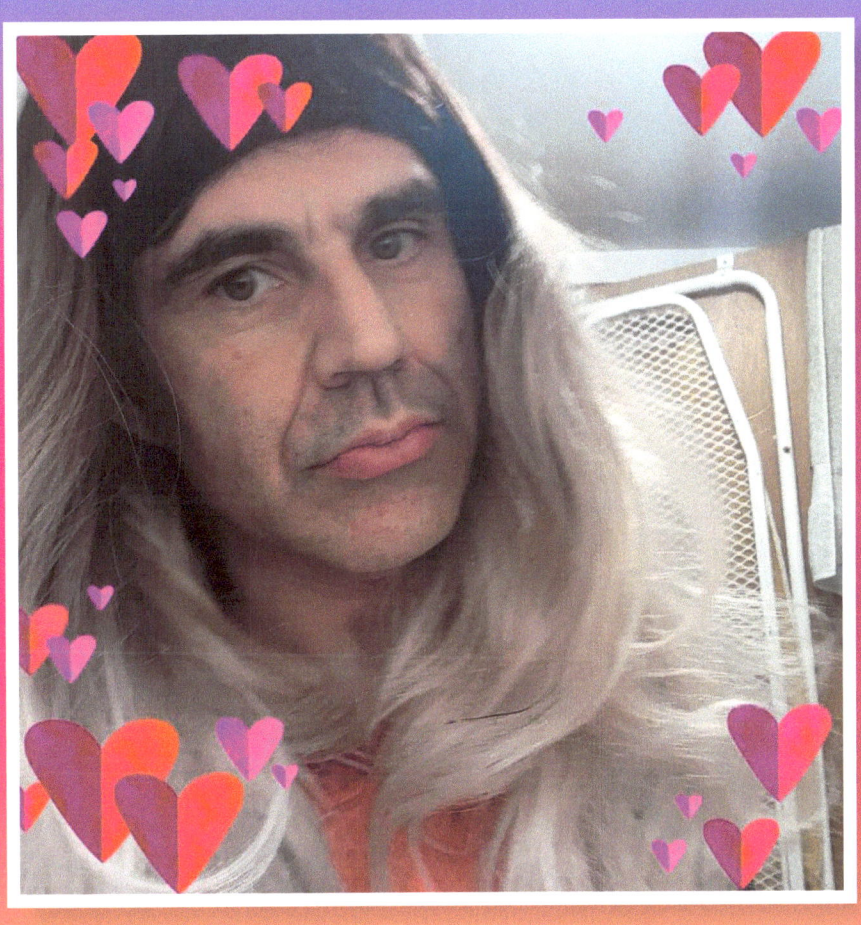

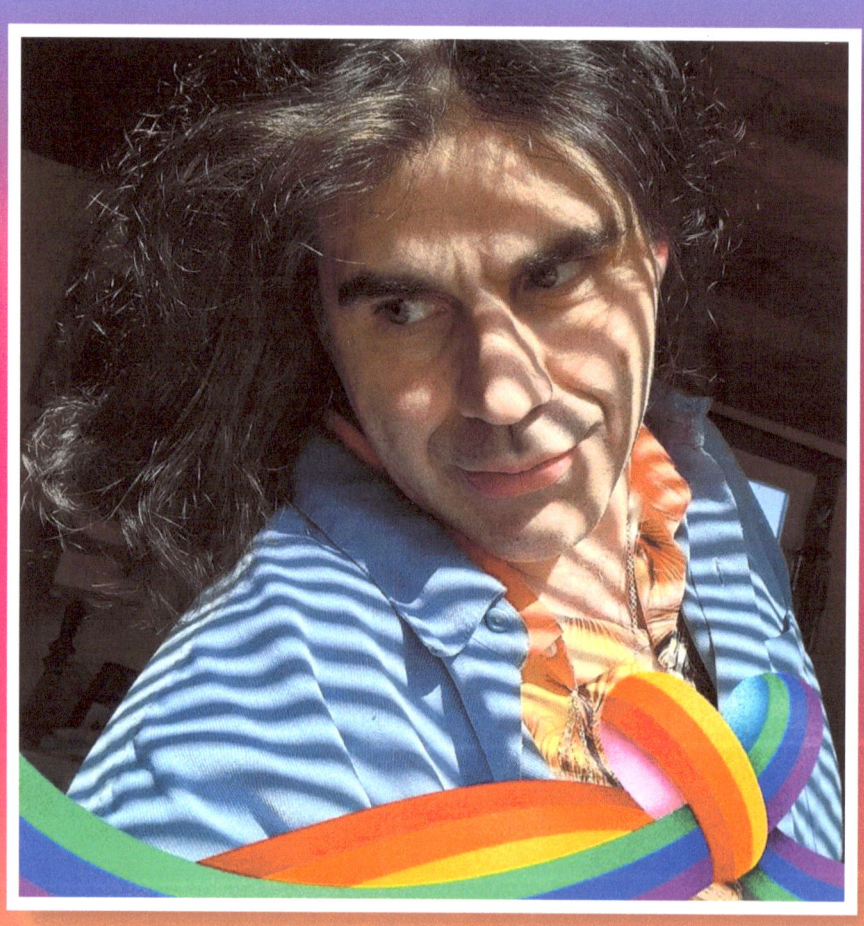

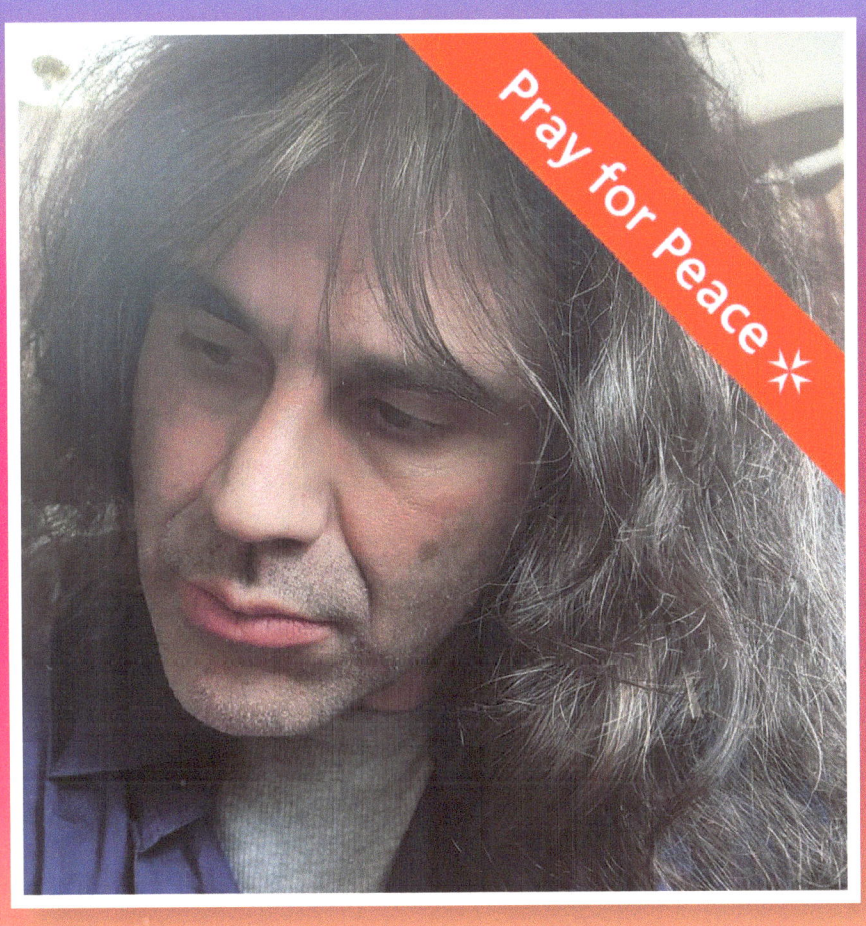

Pray for Peace ✴

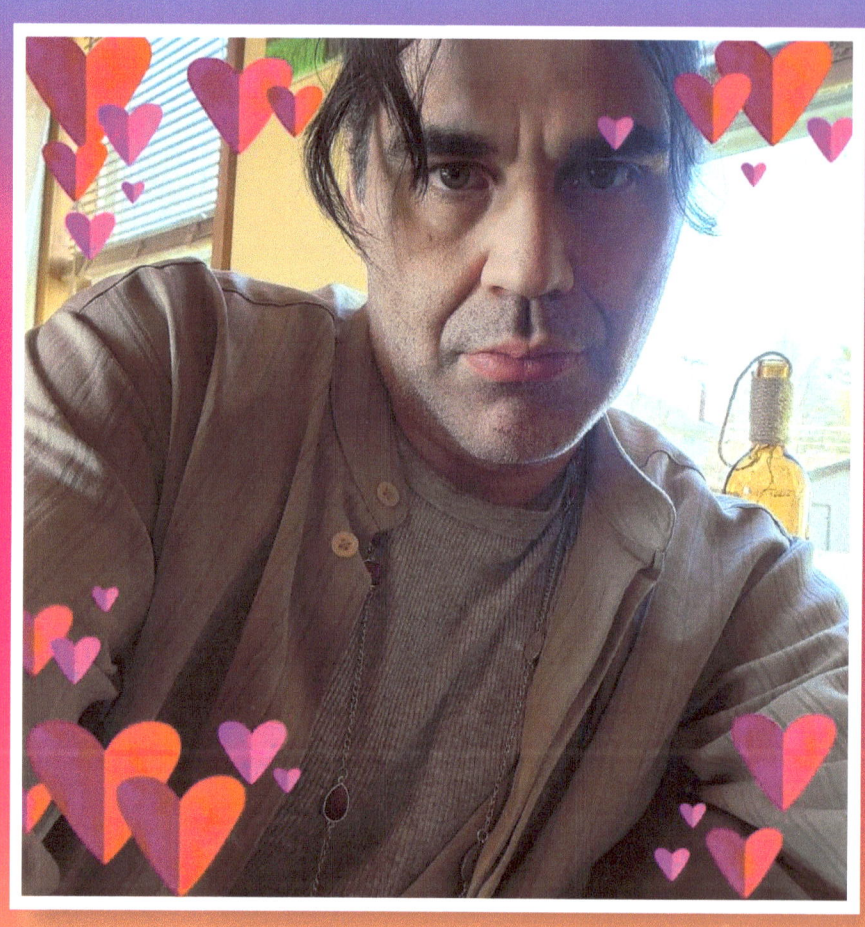

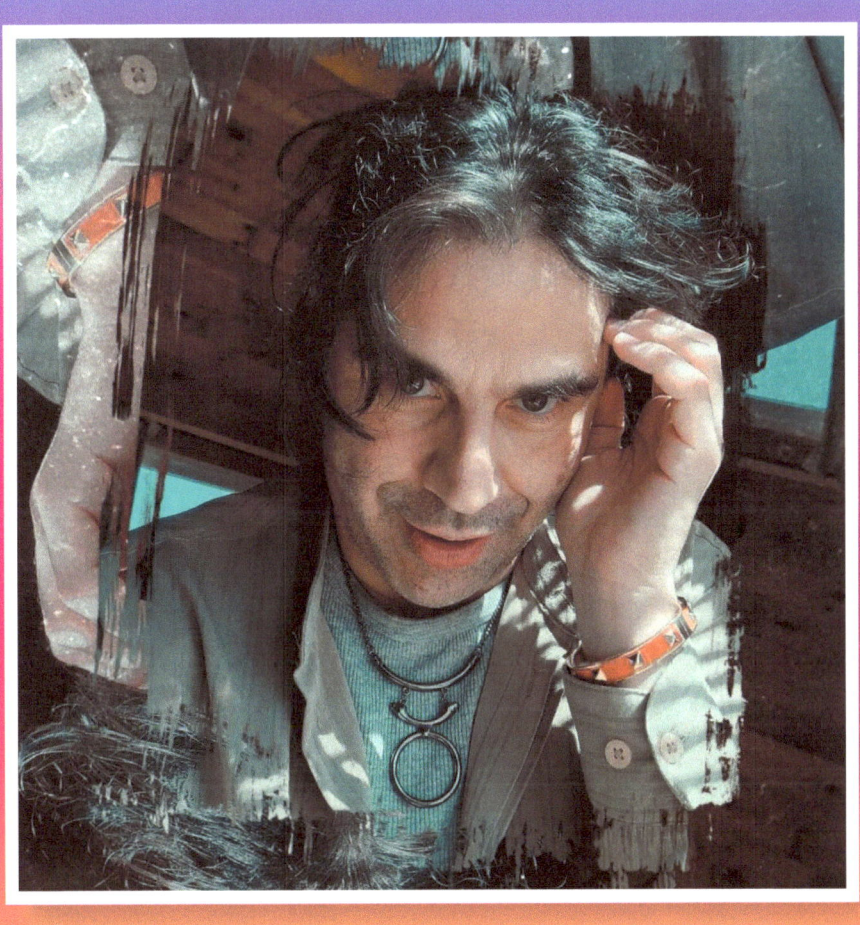

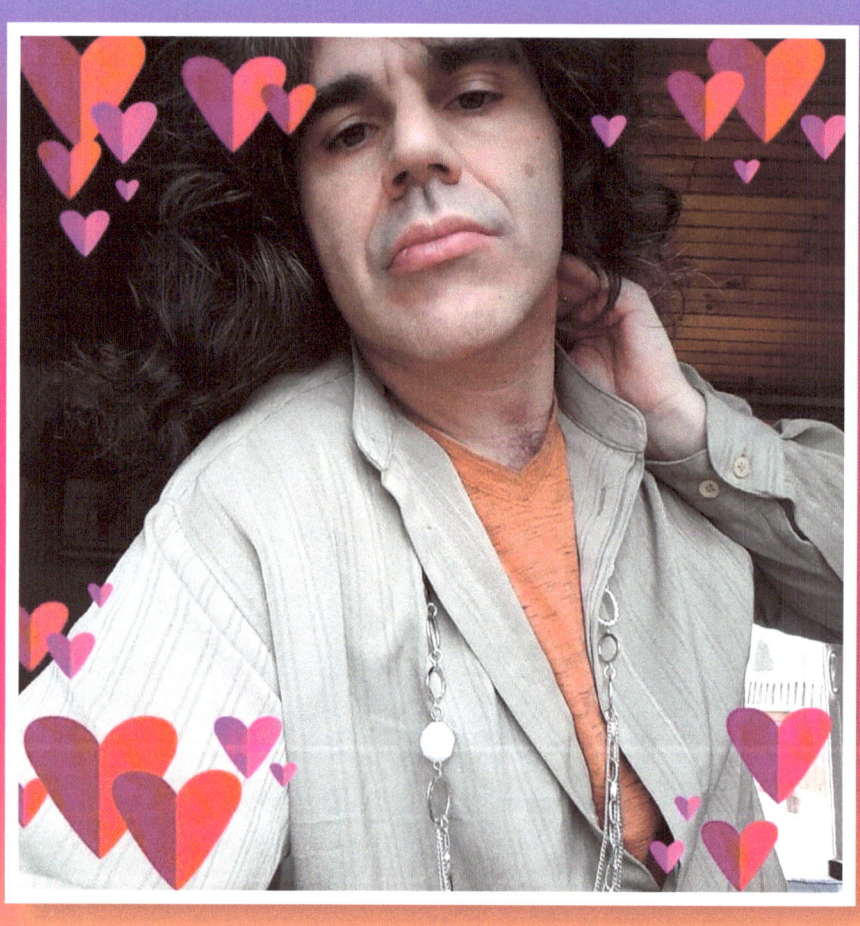

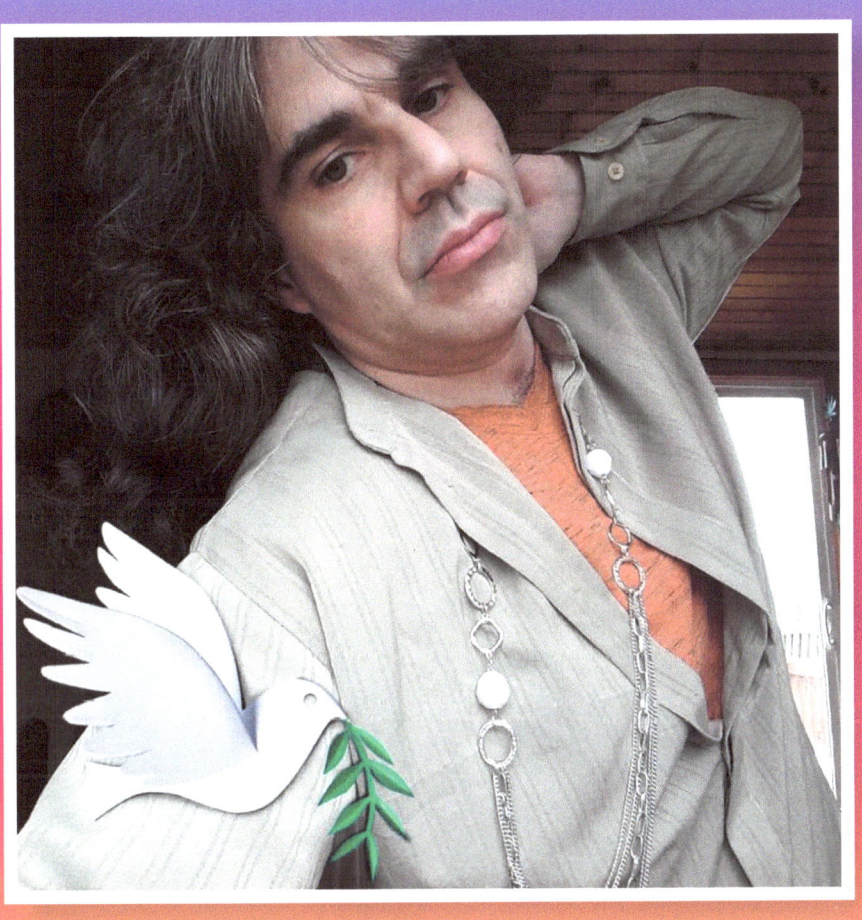

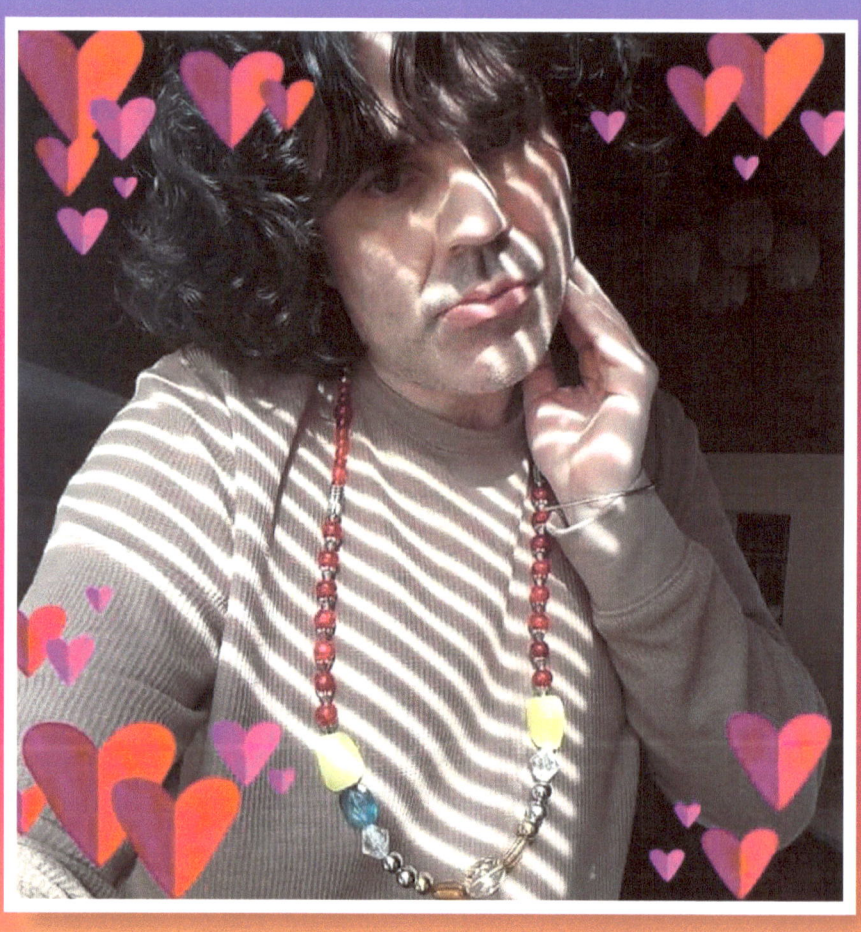

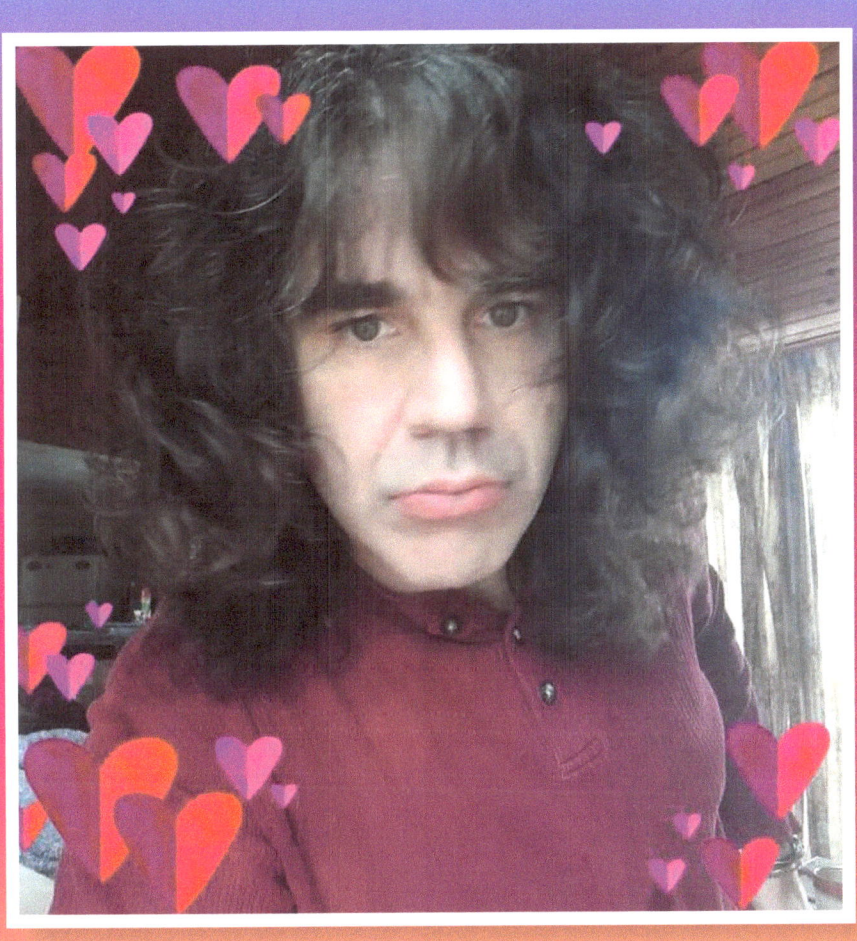

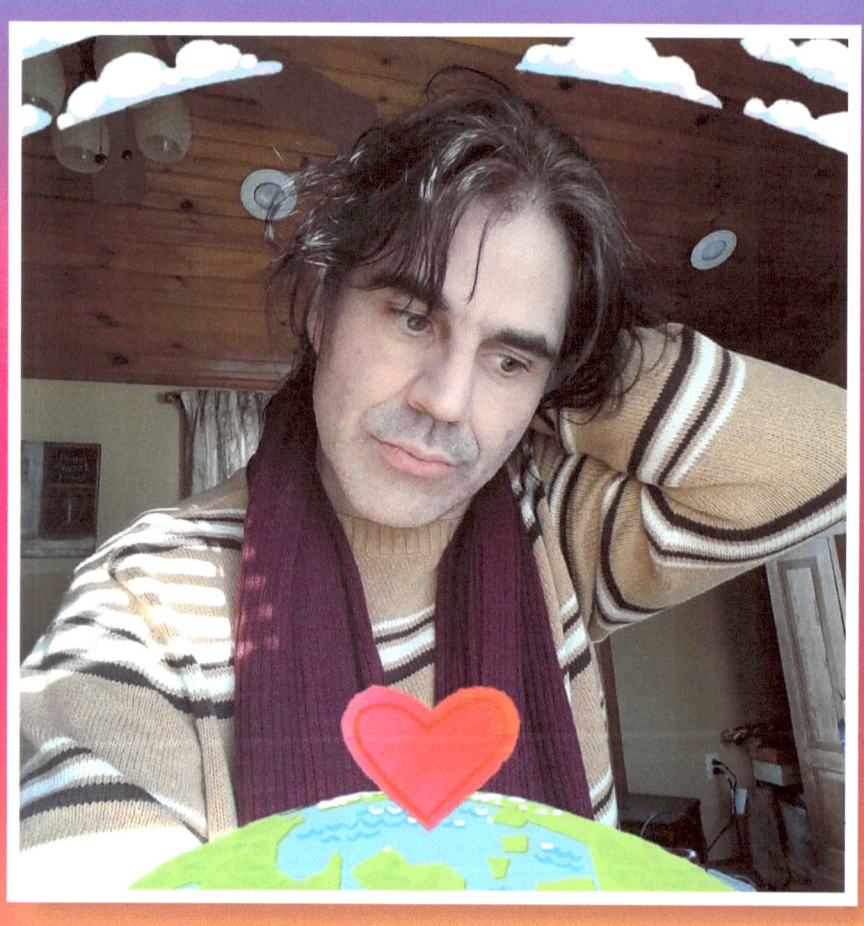

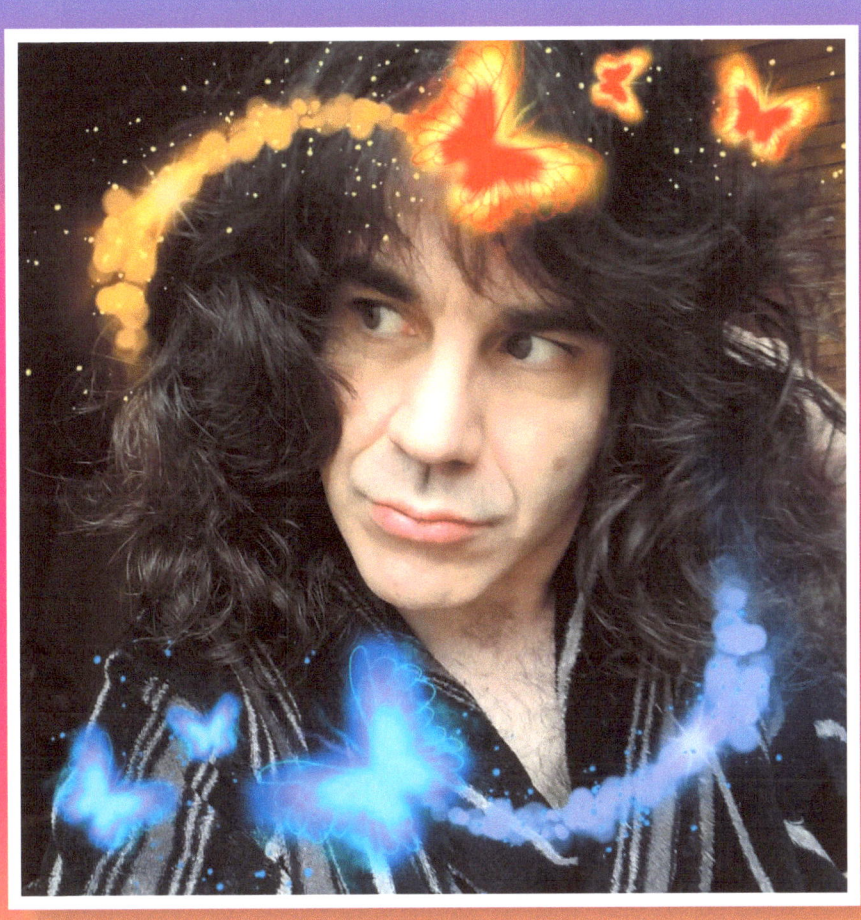

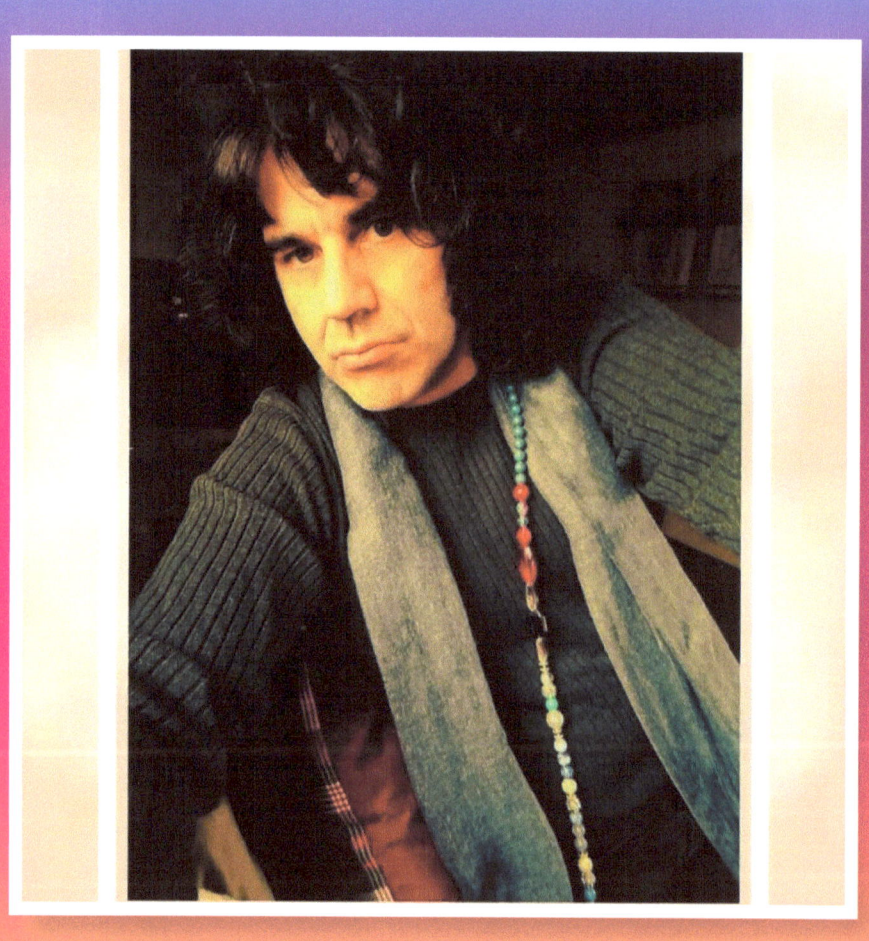

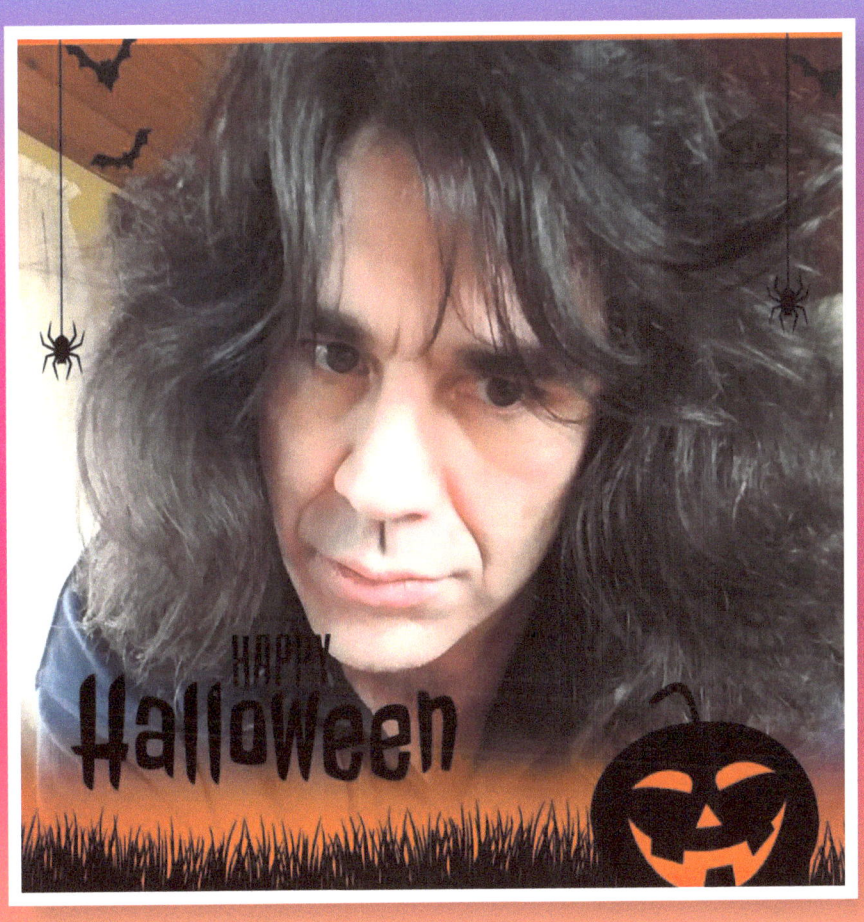

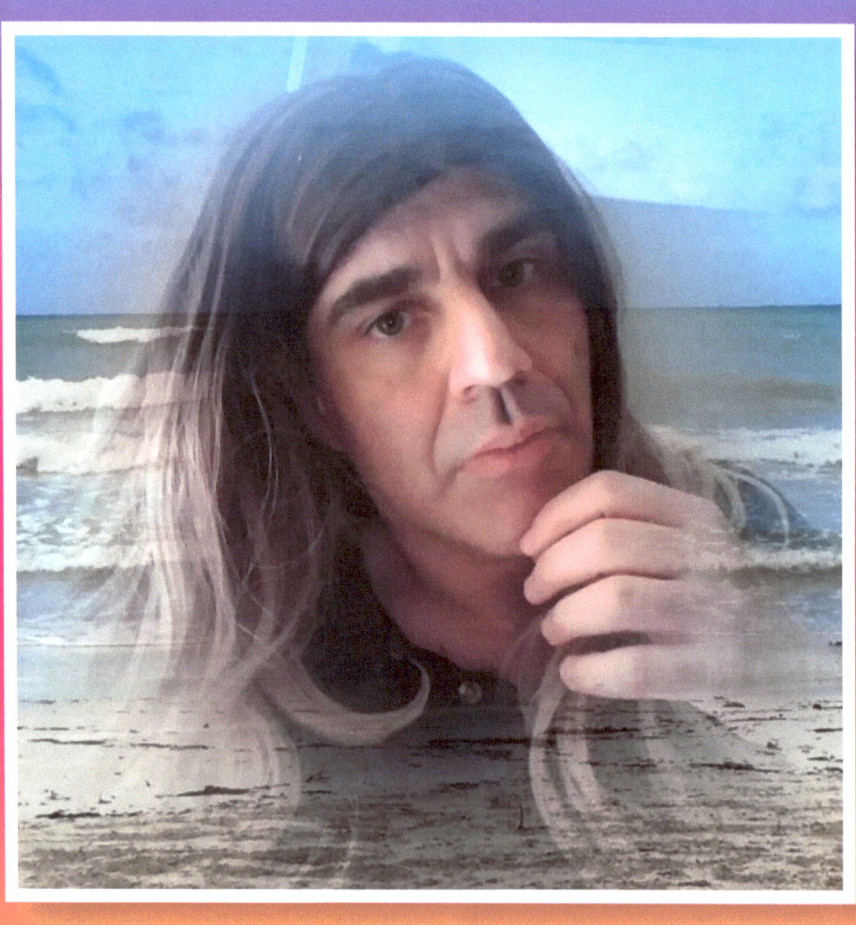

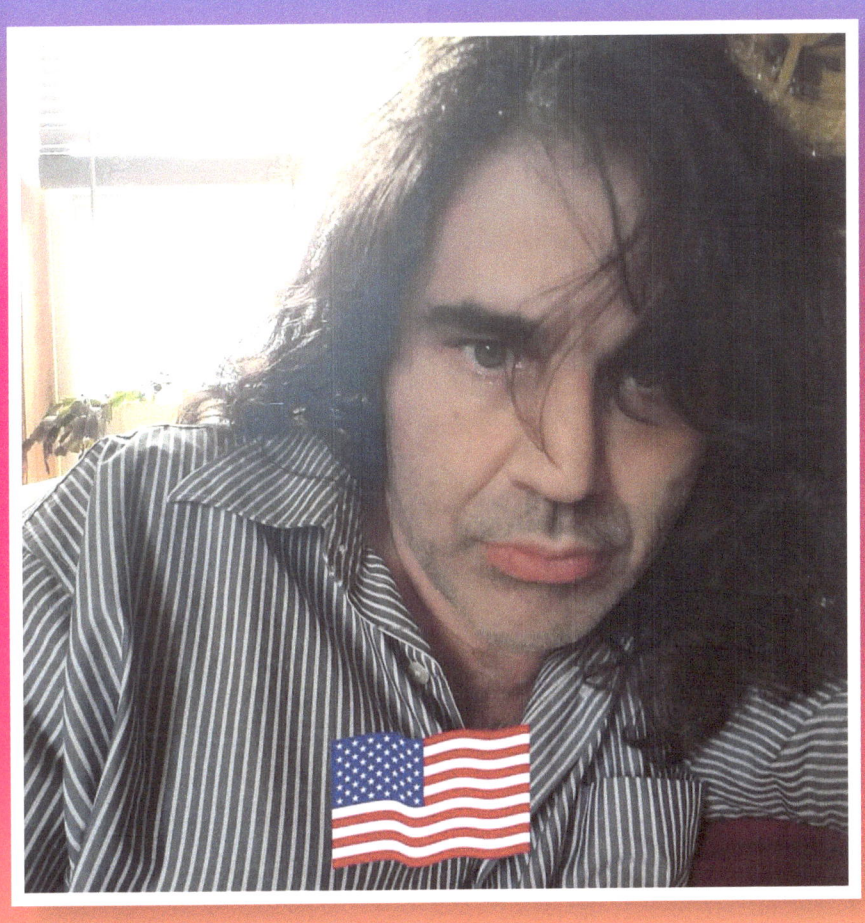

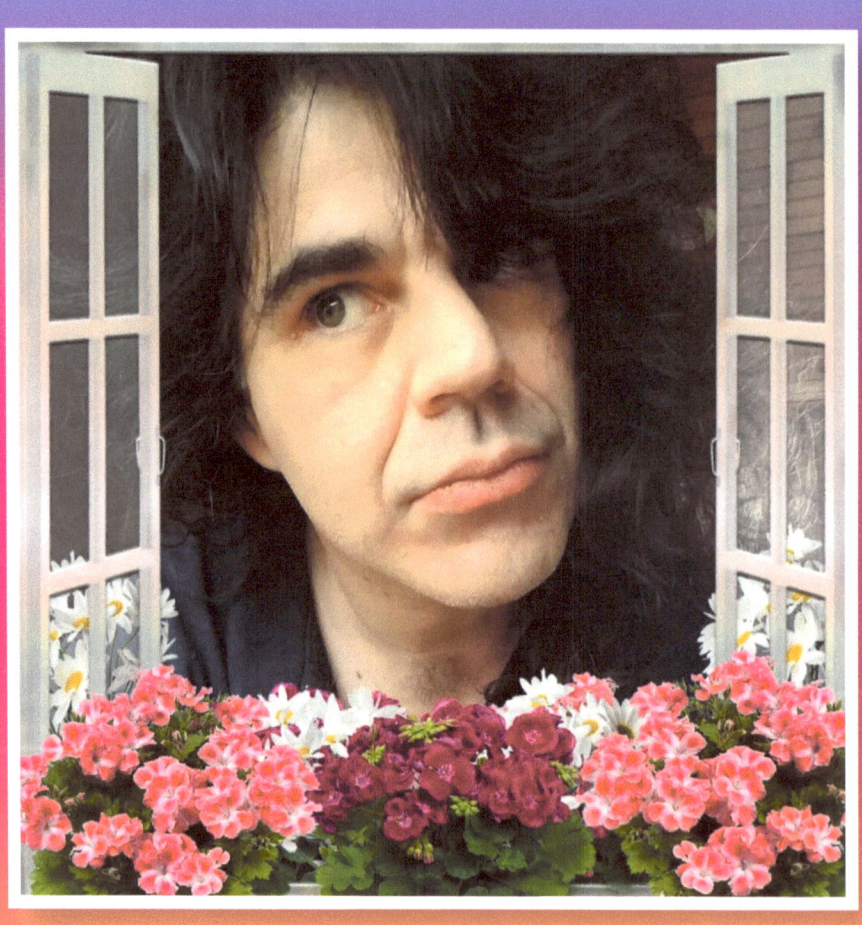

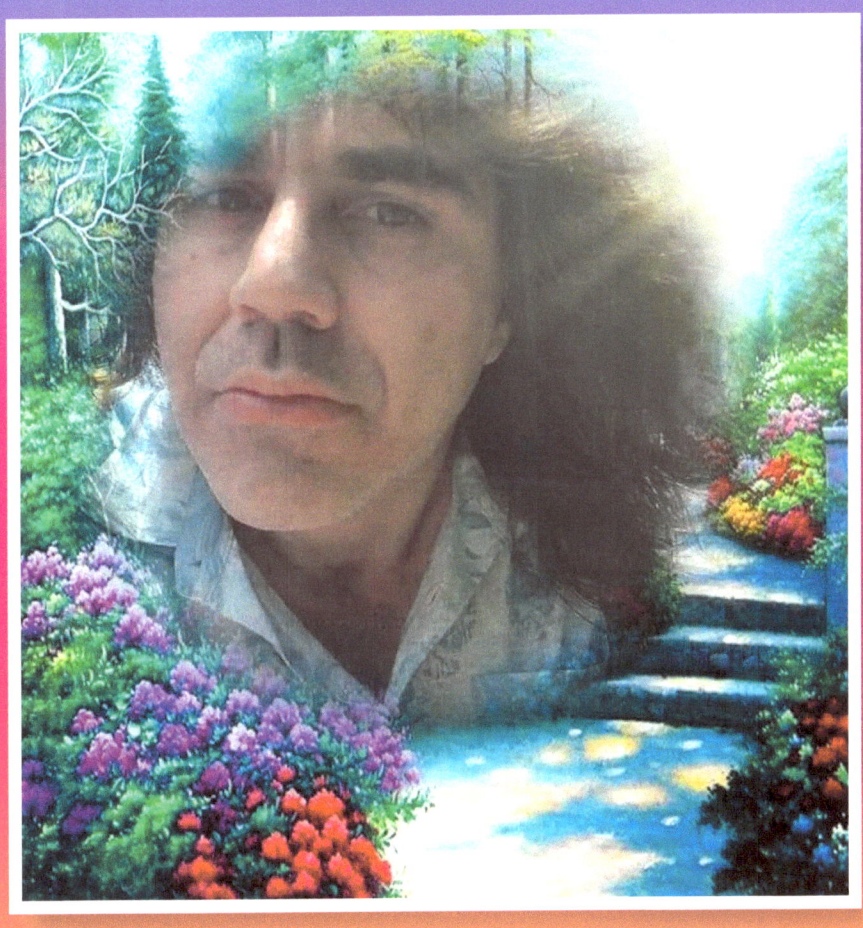

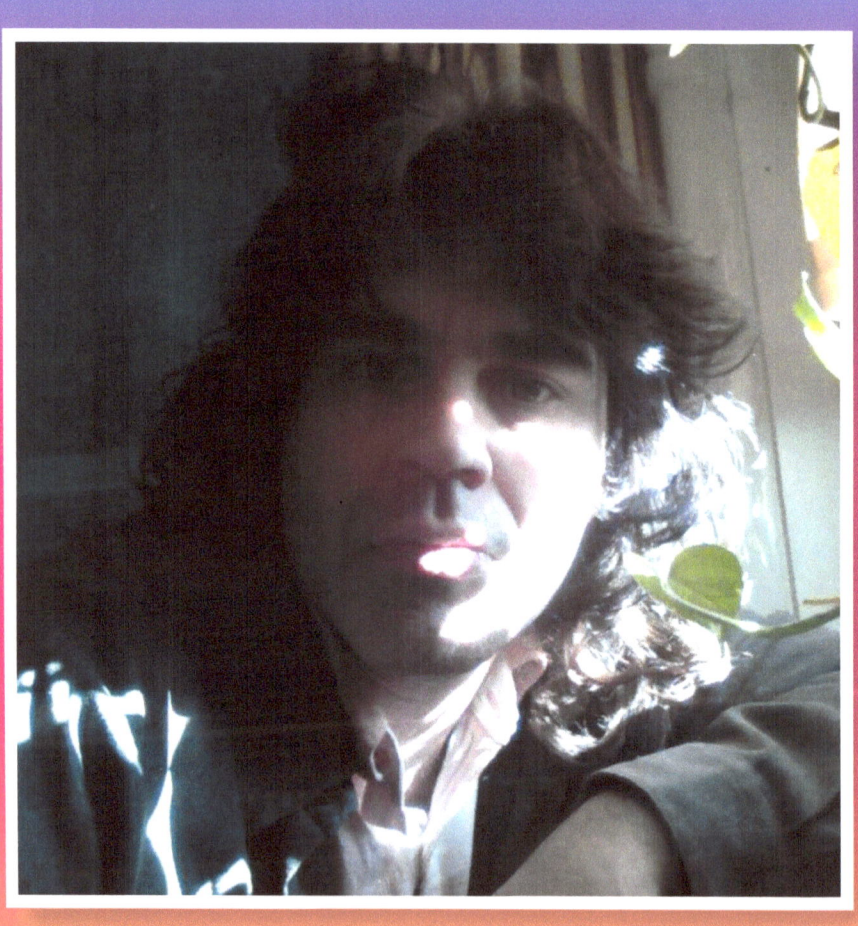

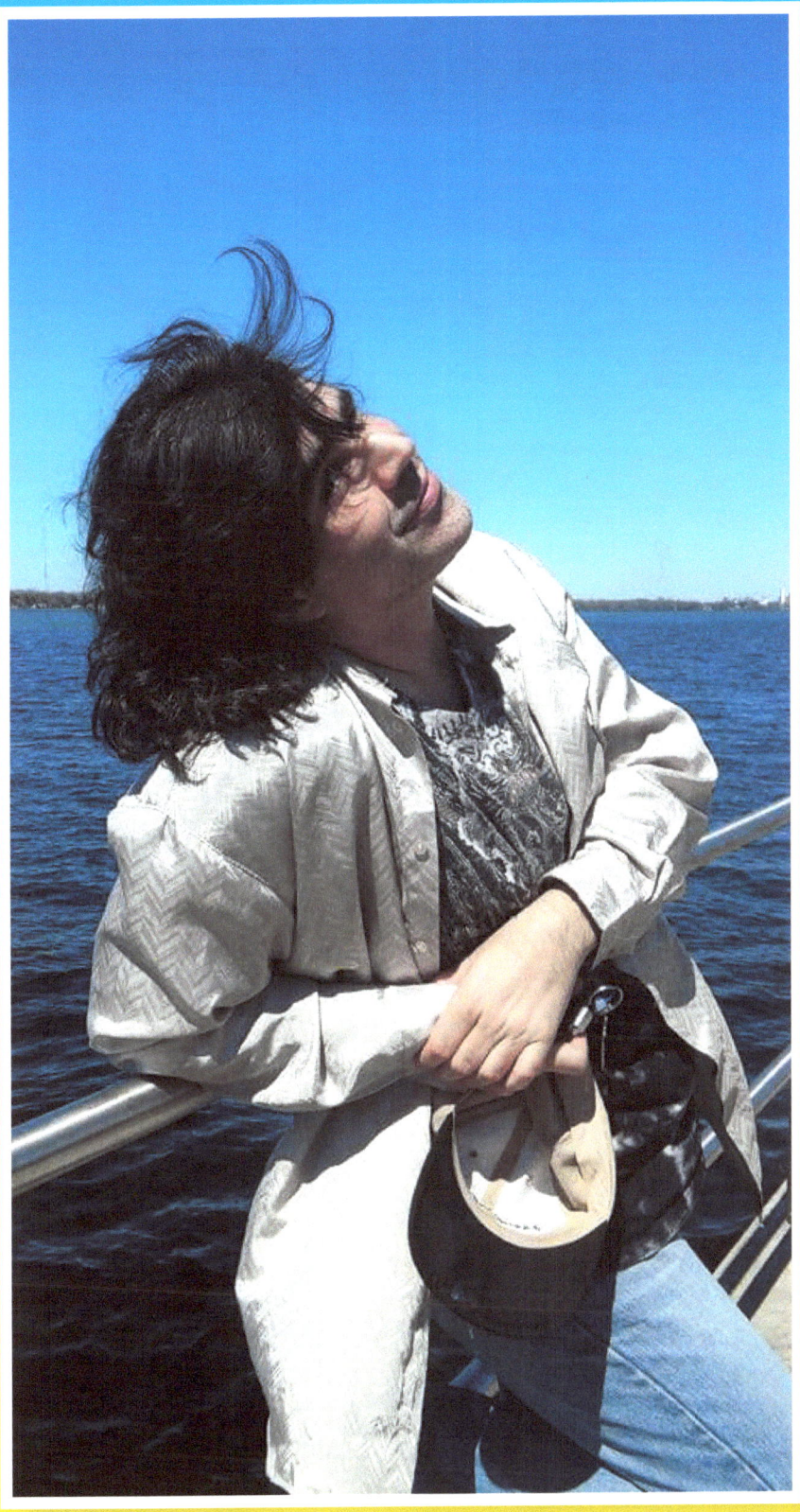

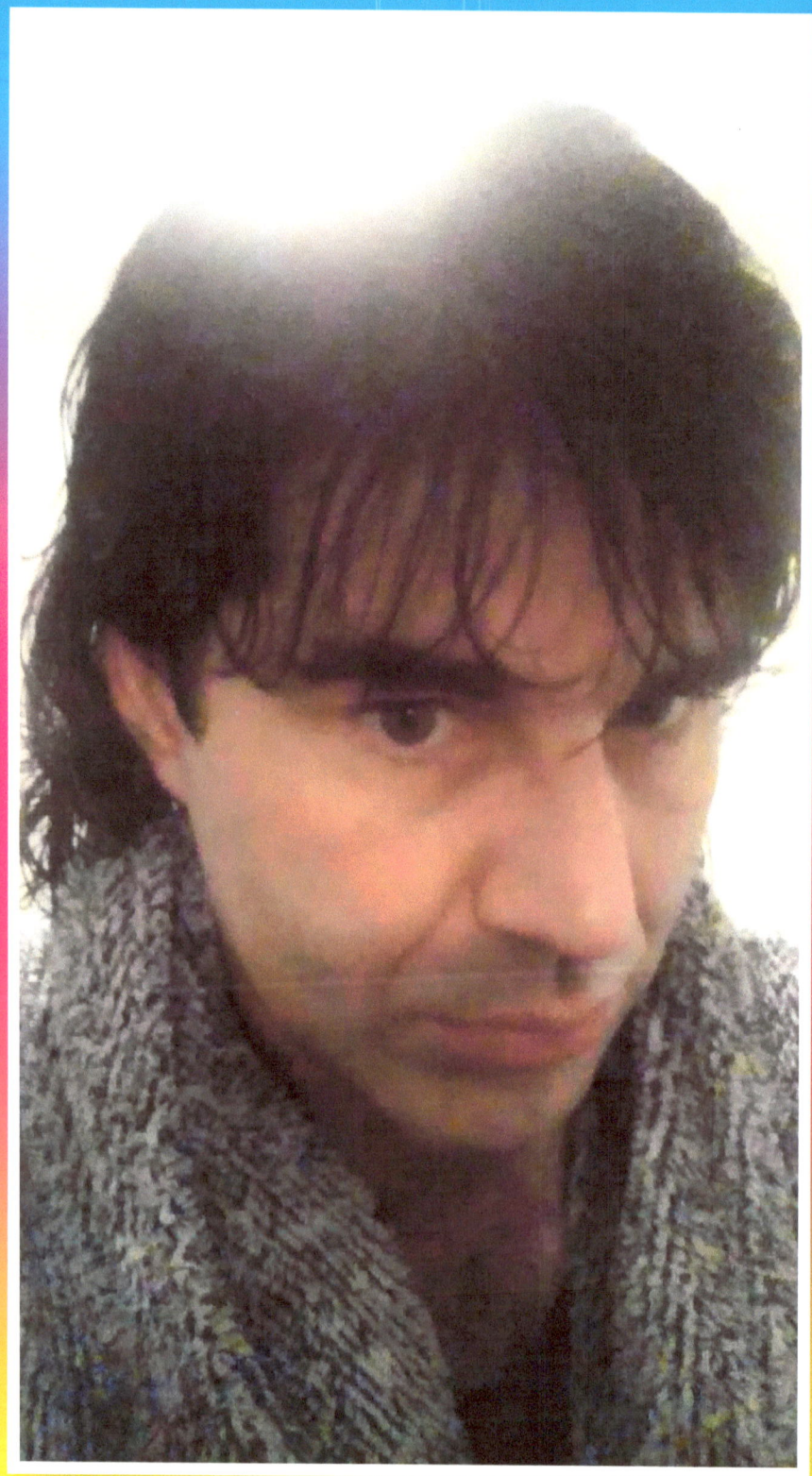

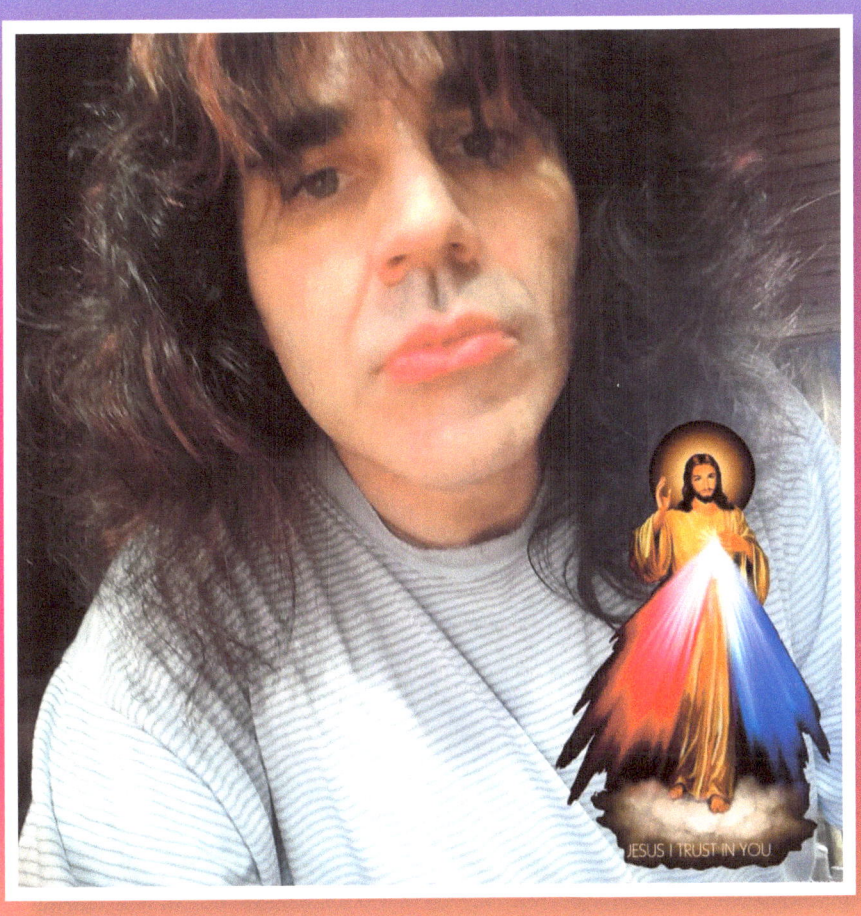

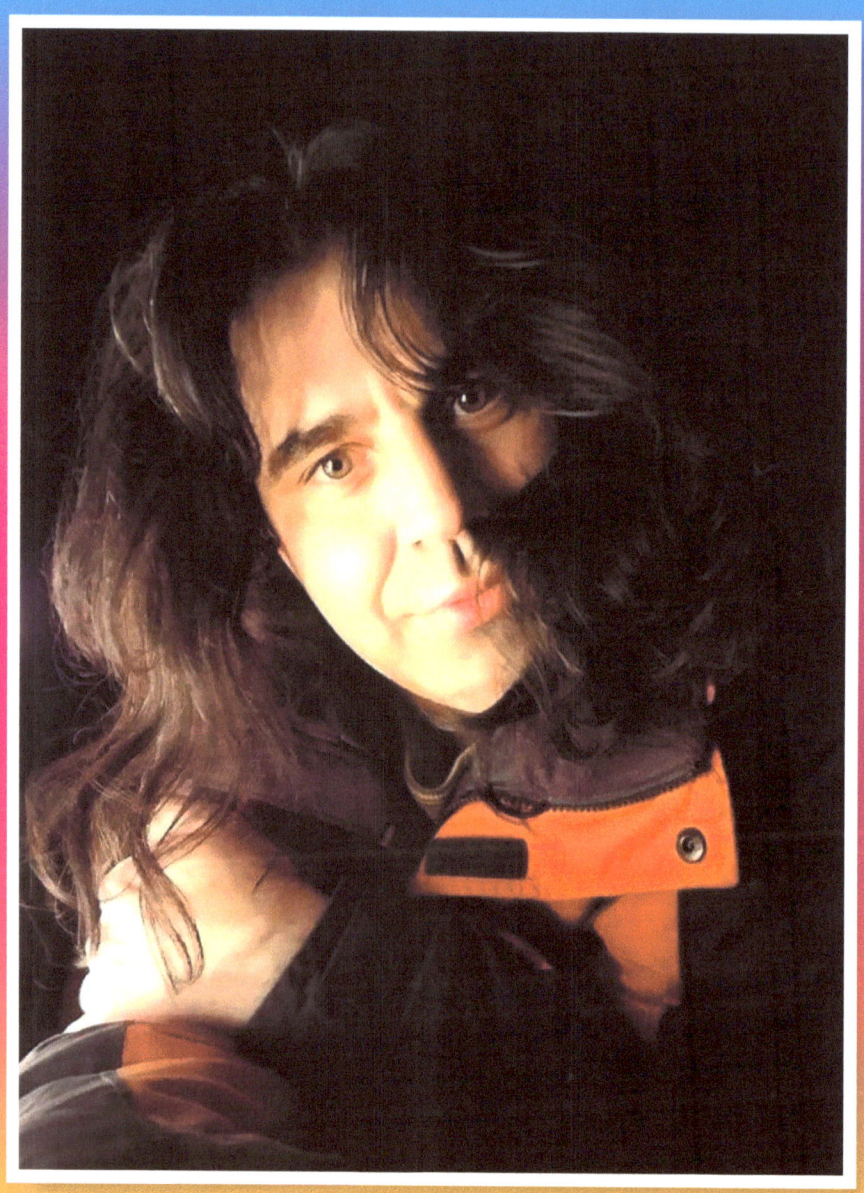

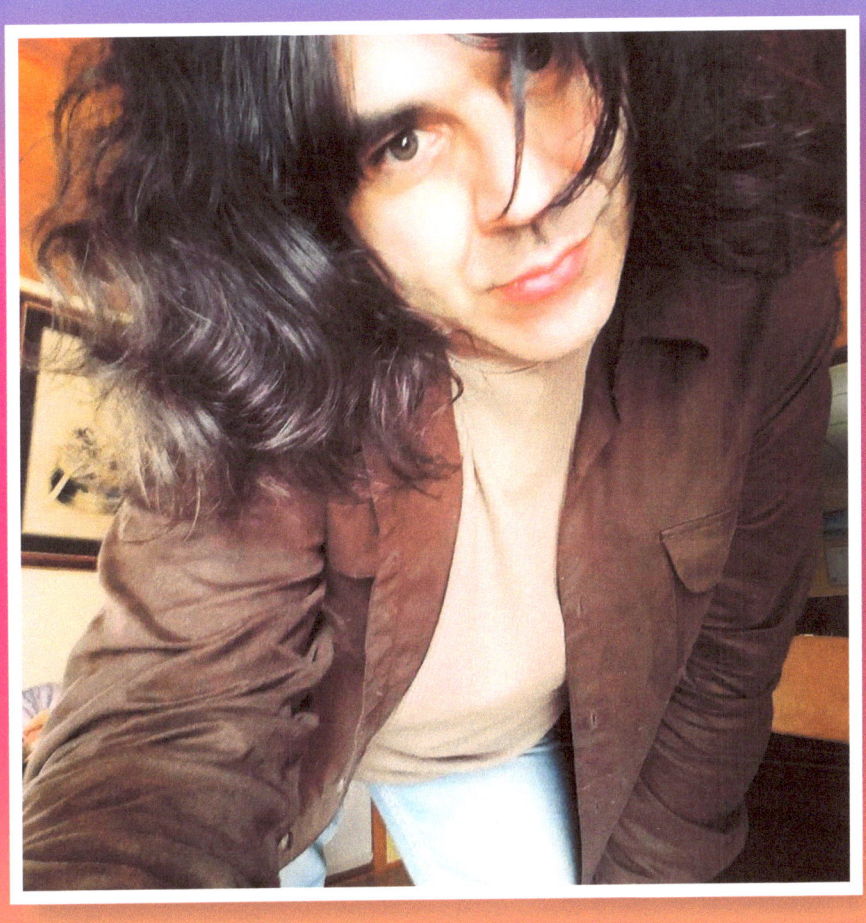

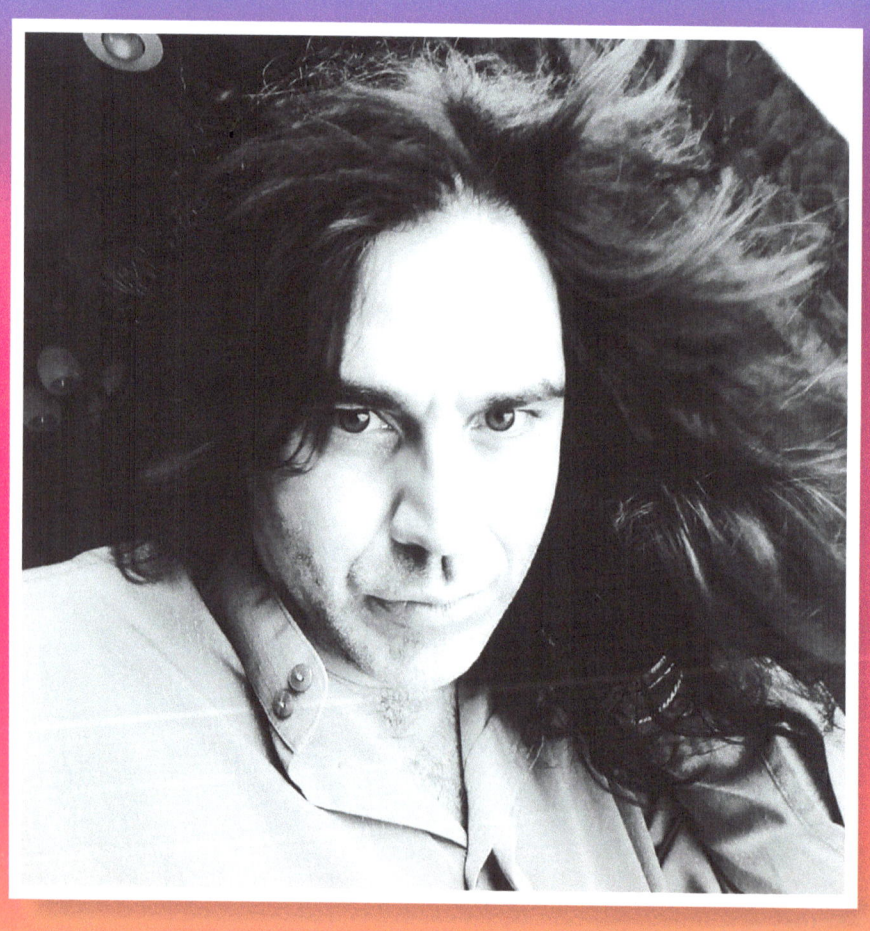

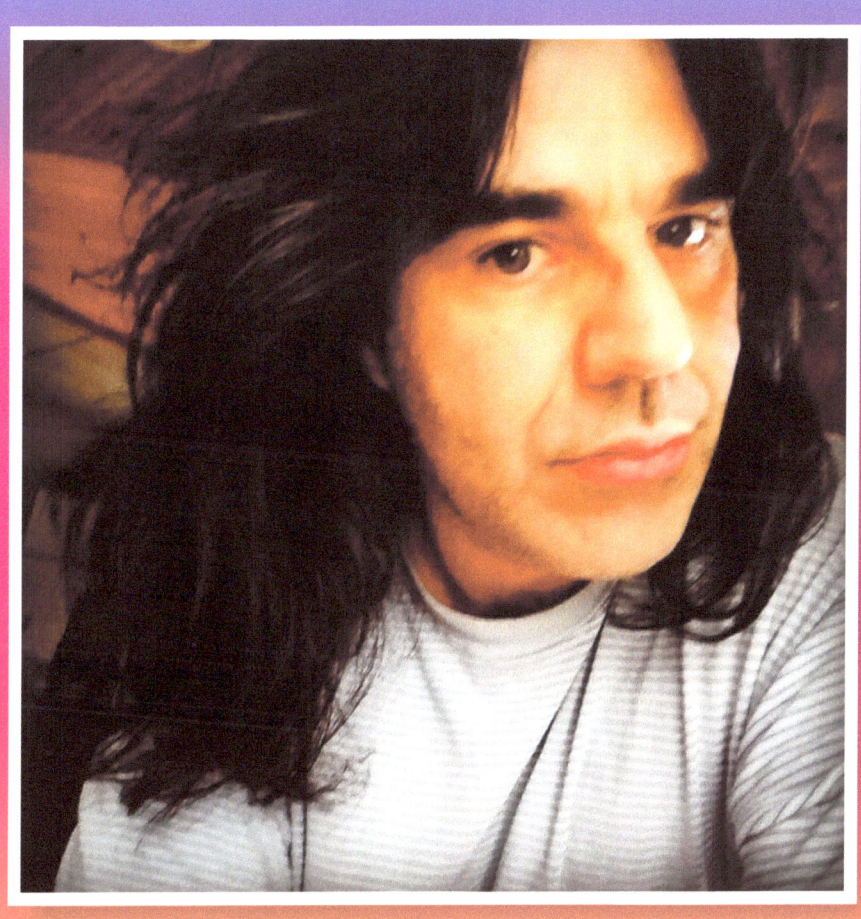

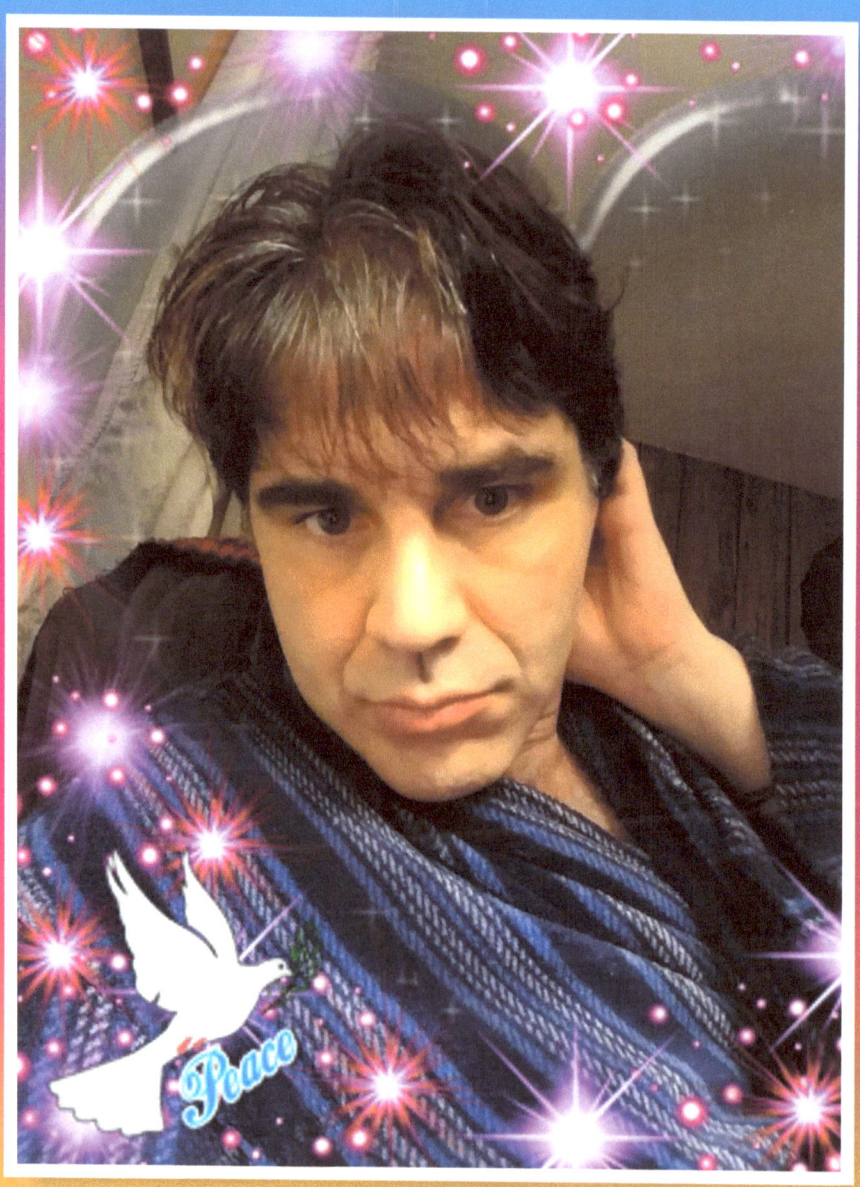
Peace

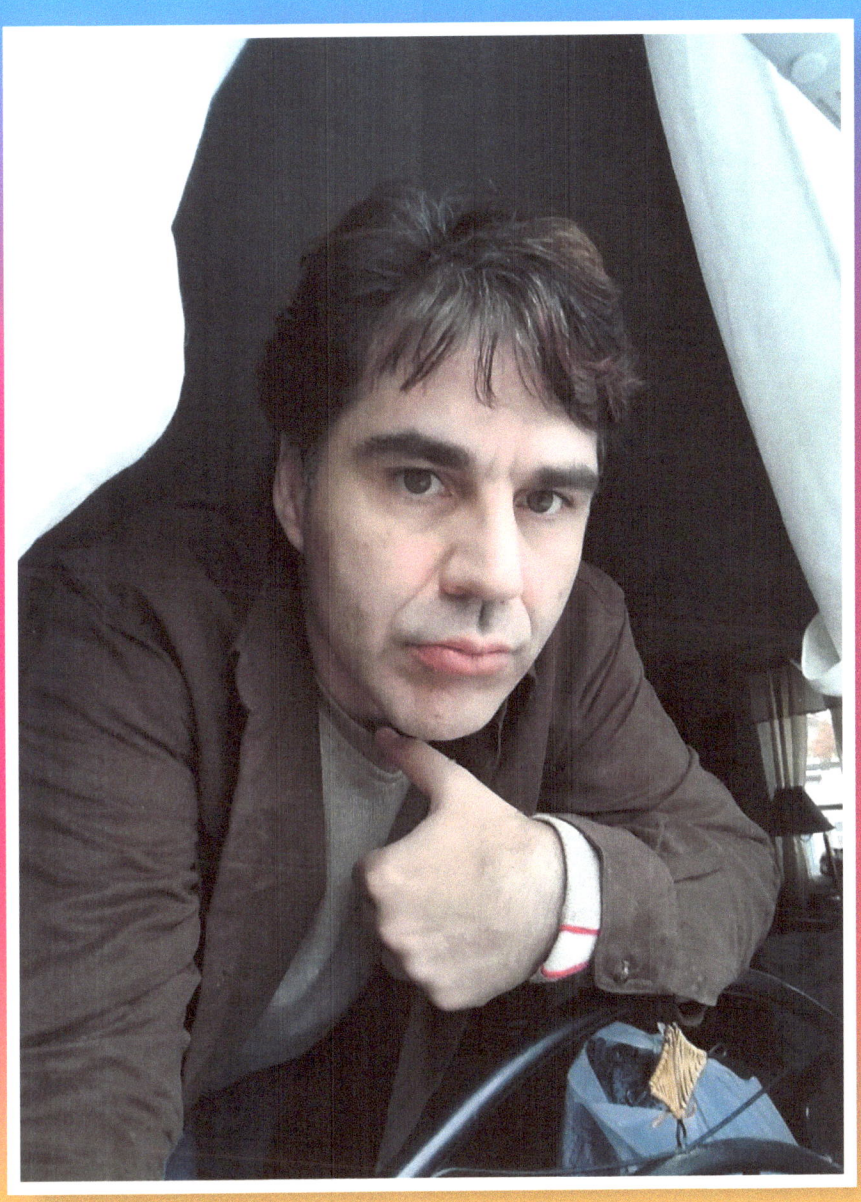

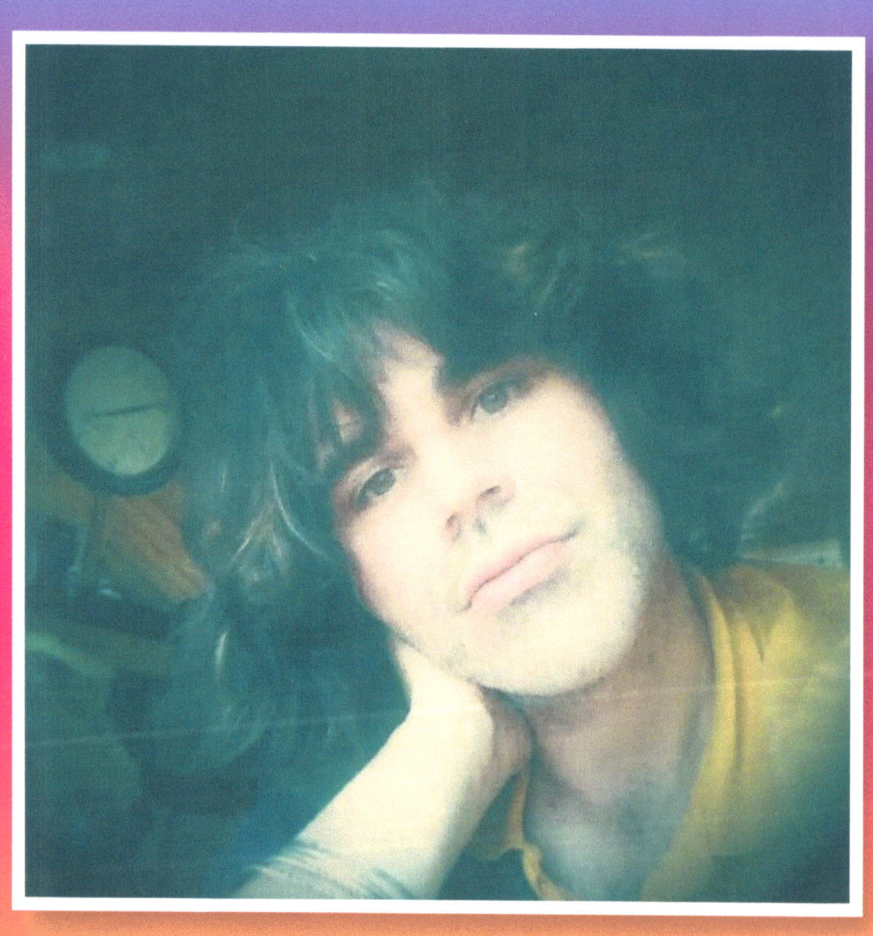

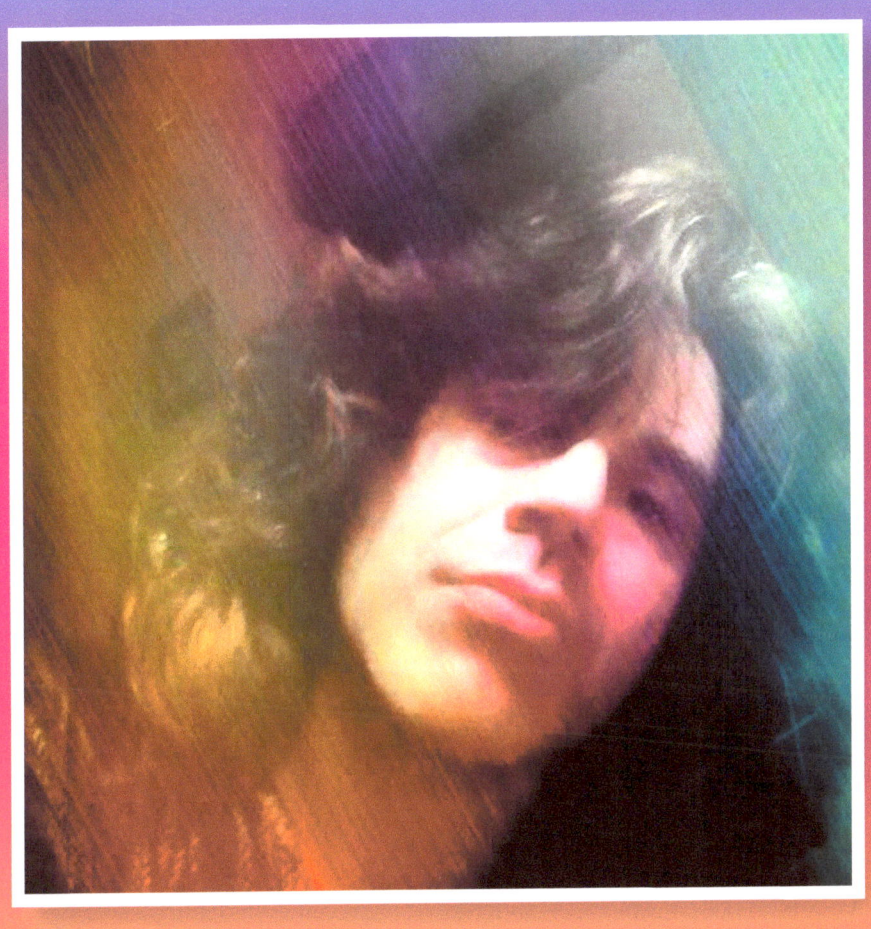

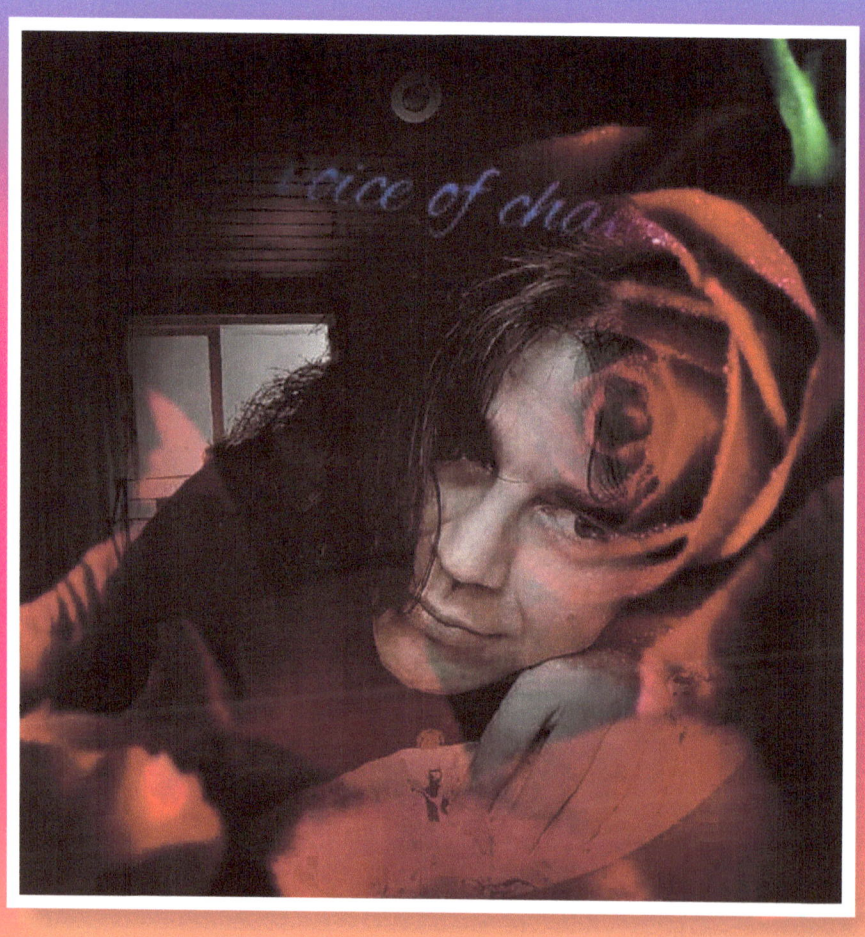

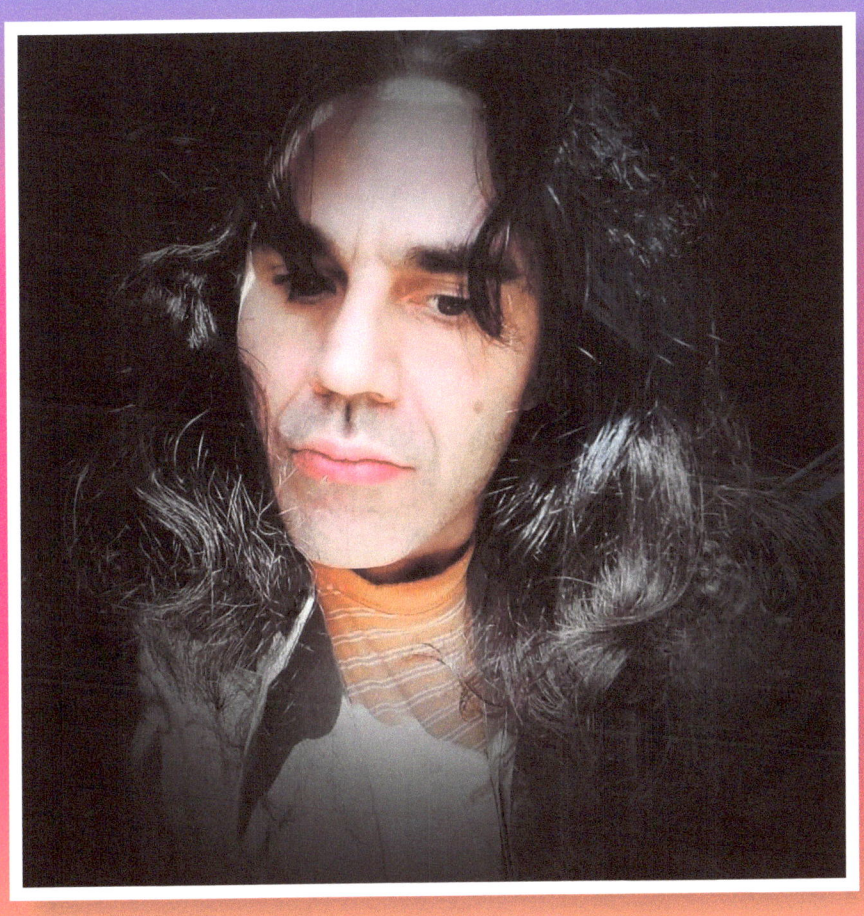

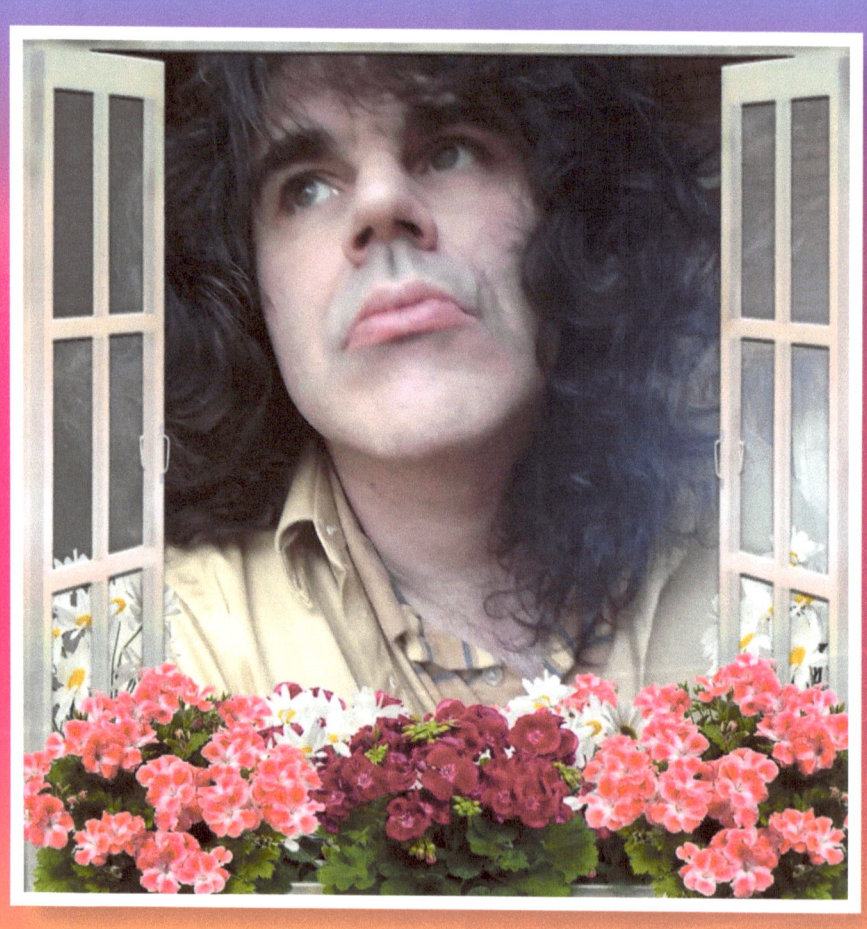

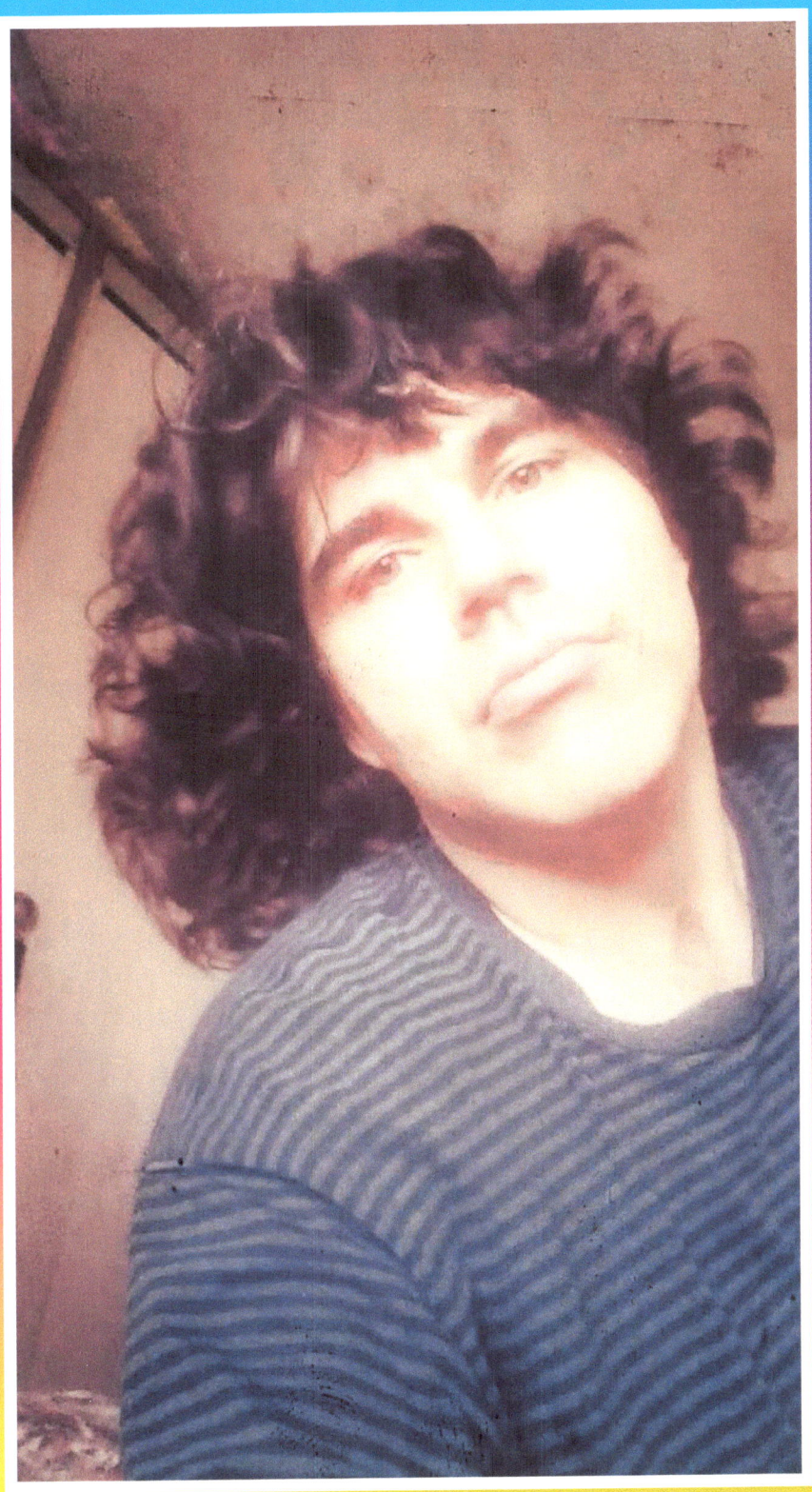

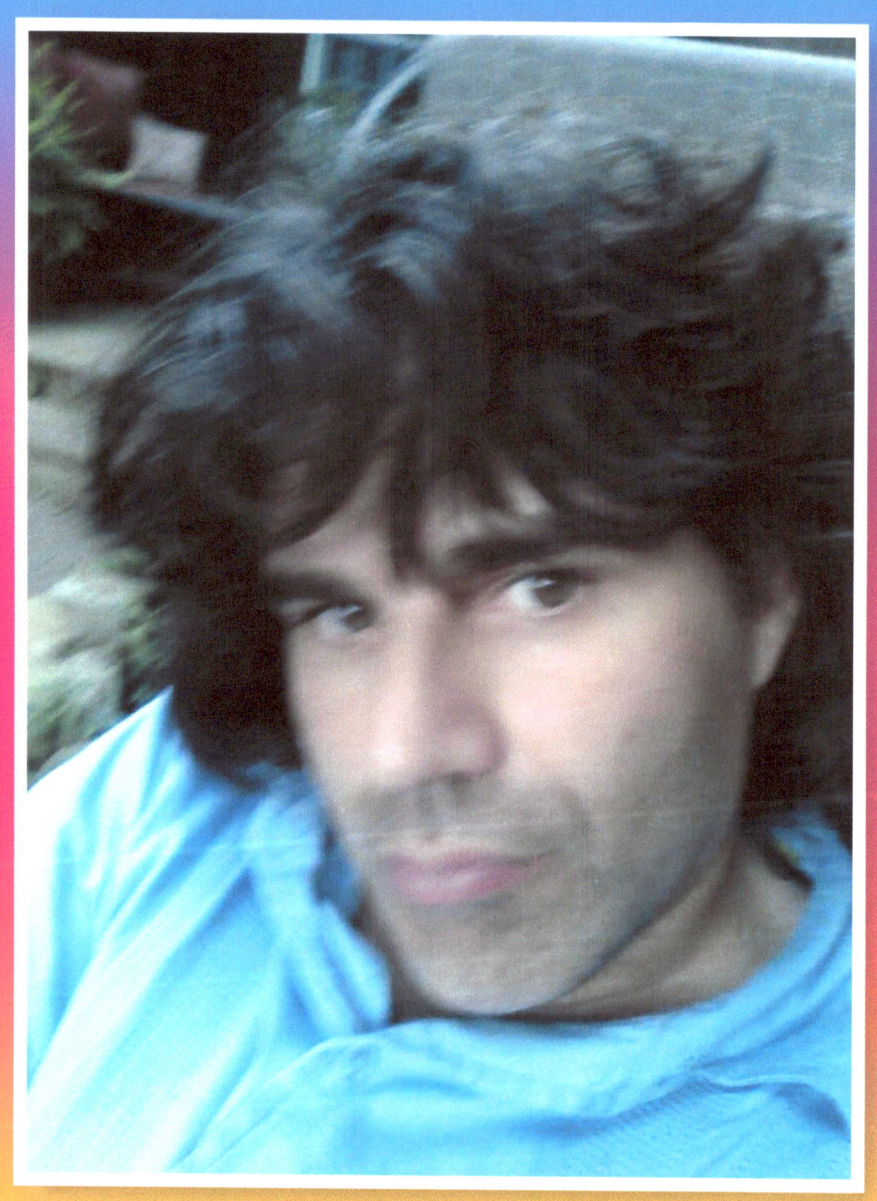

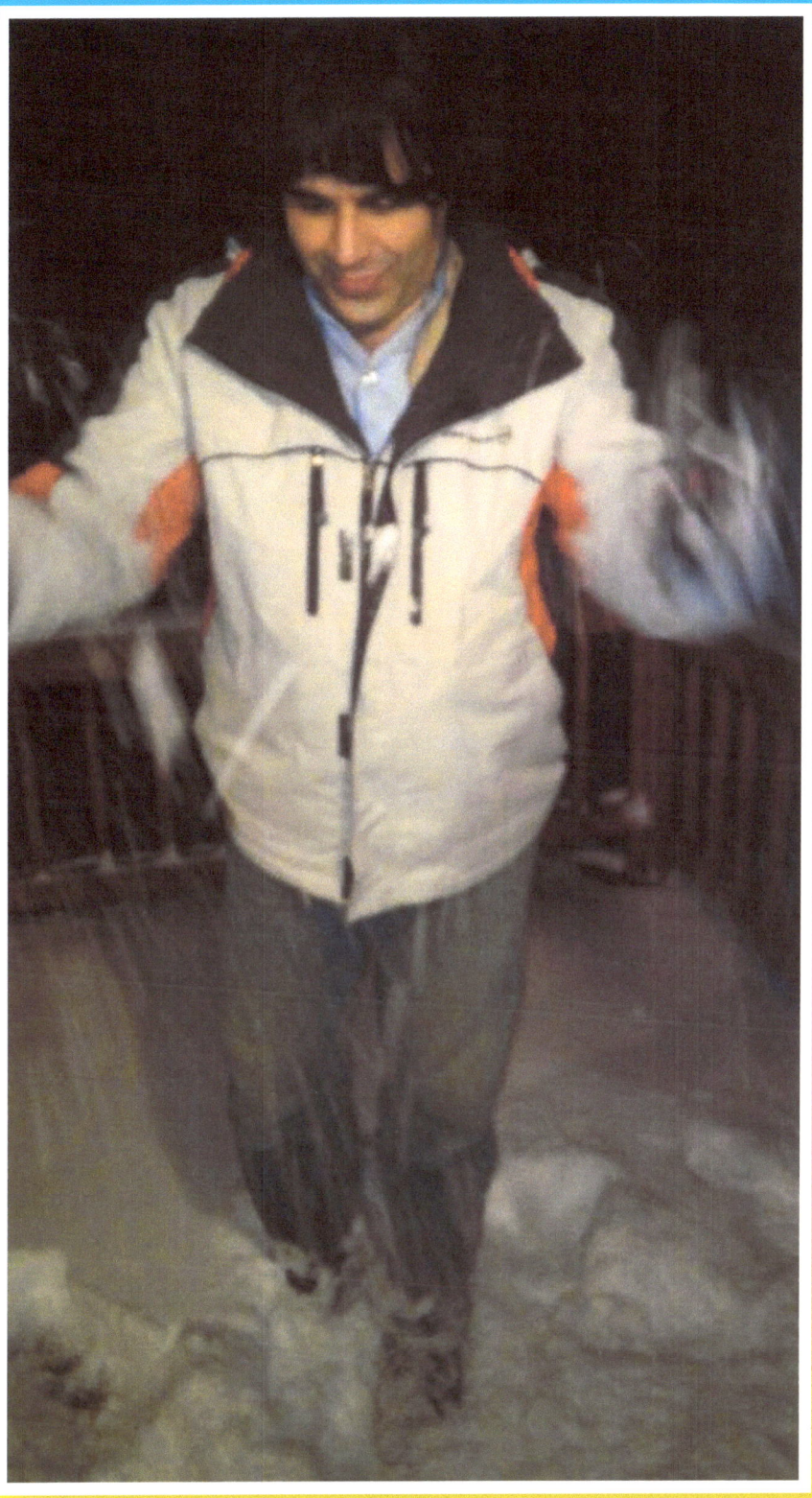

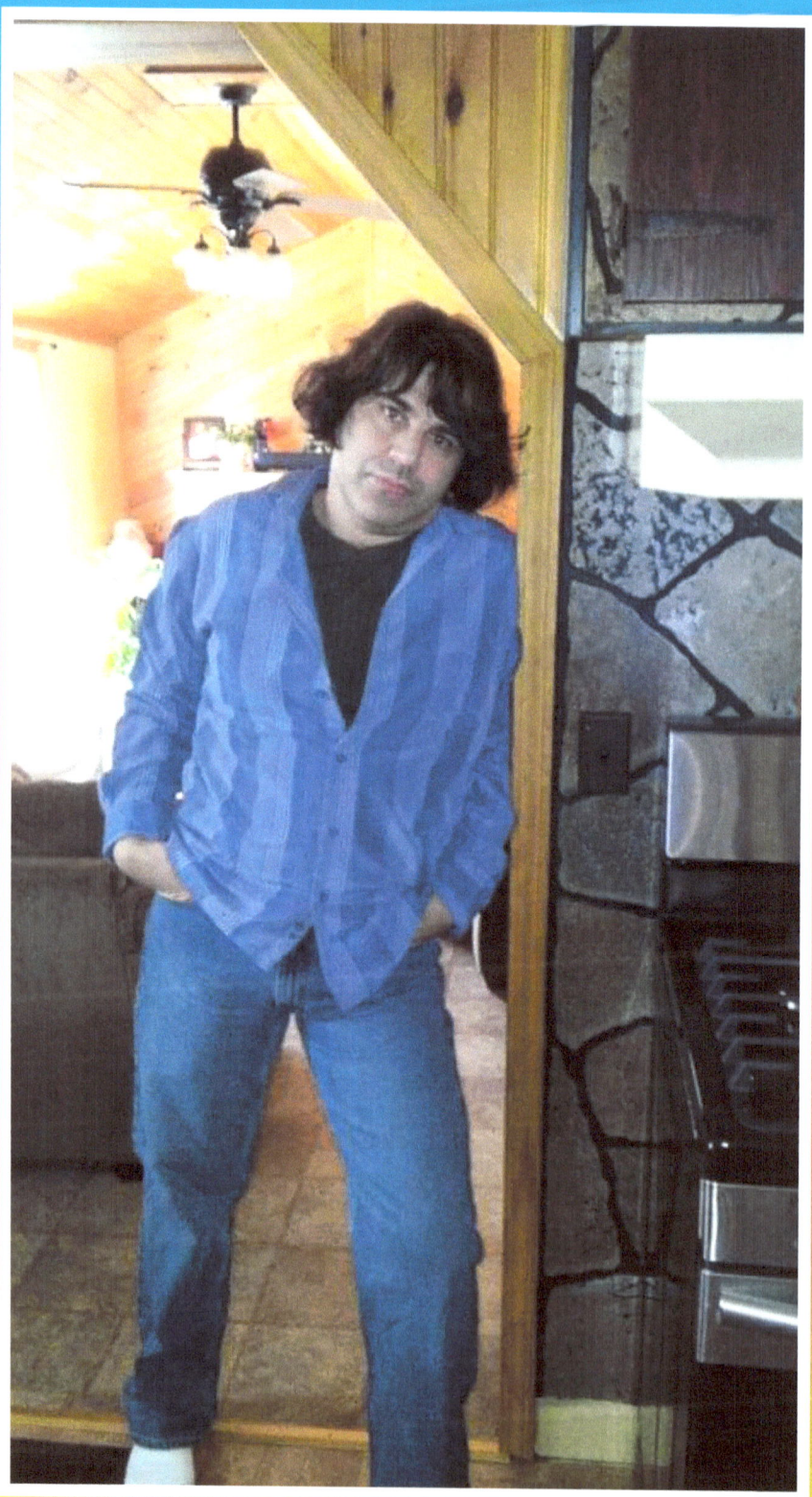

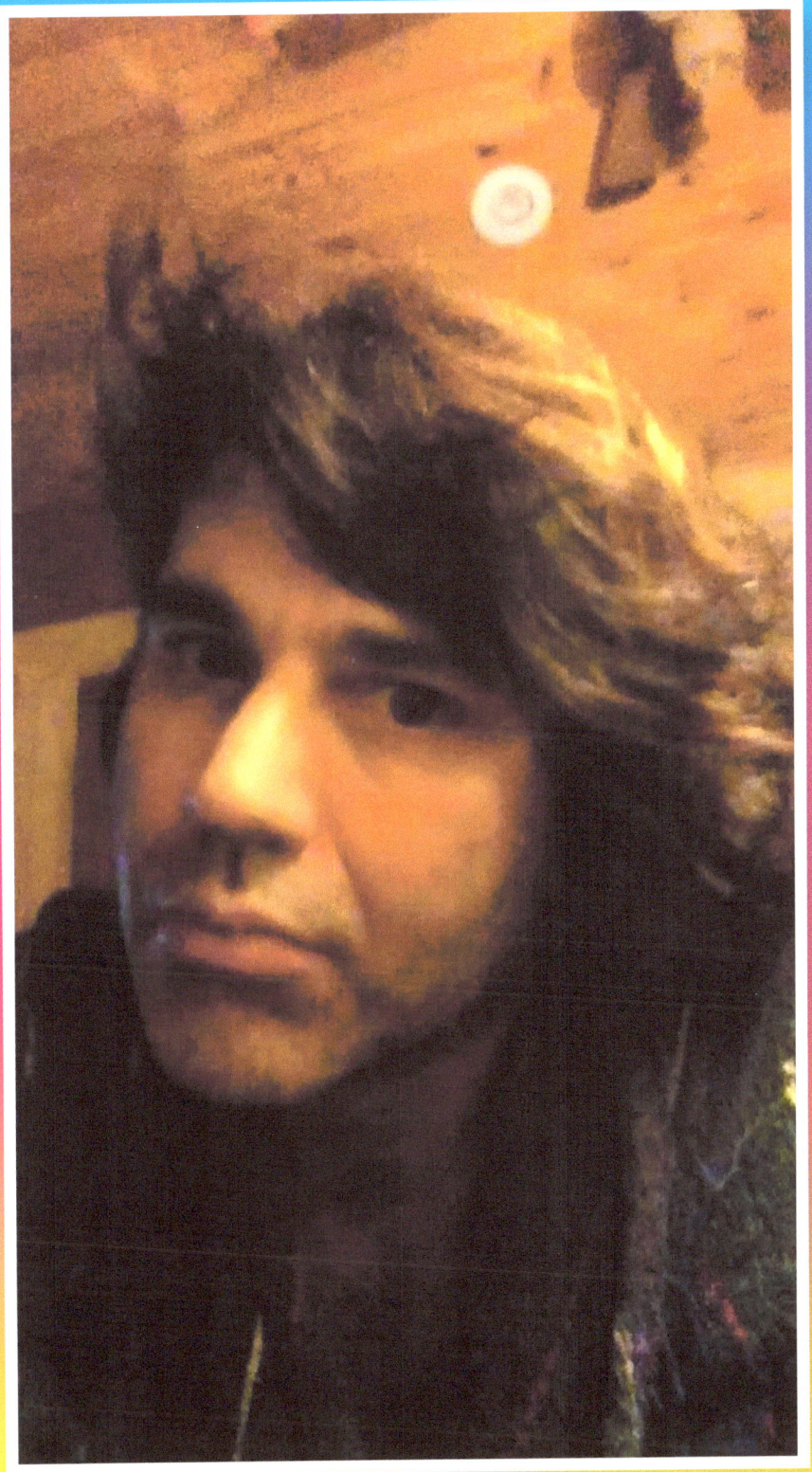

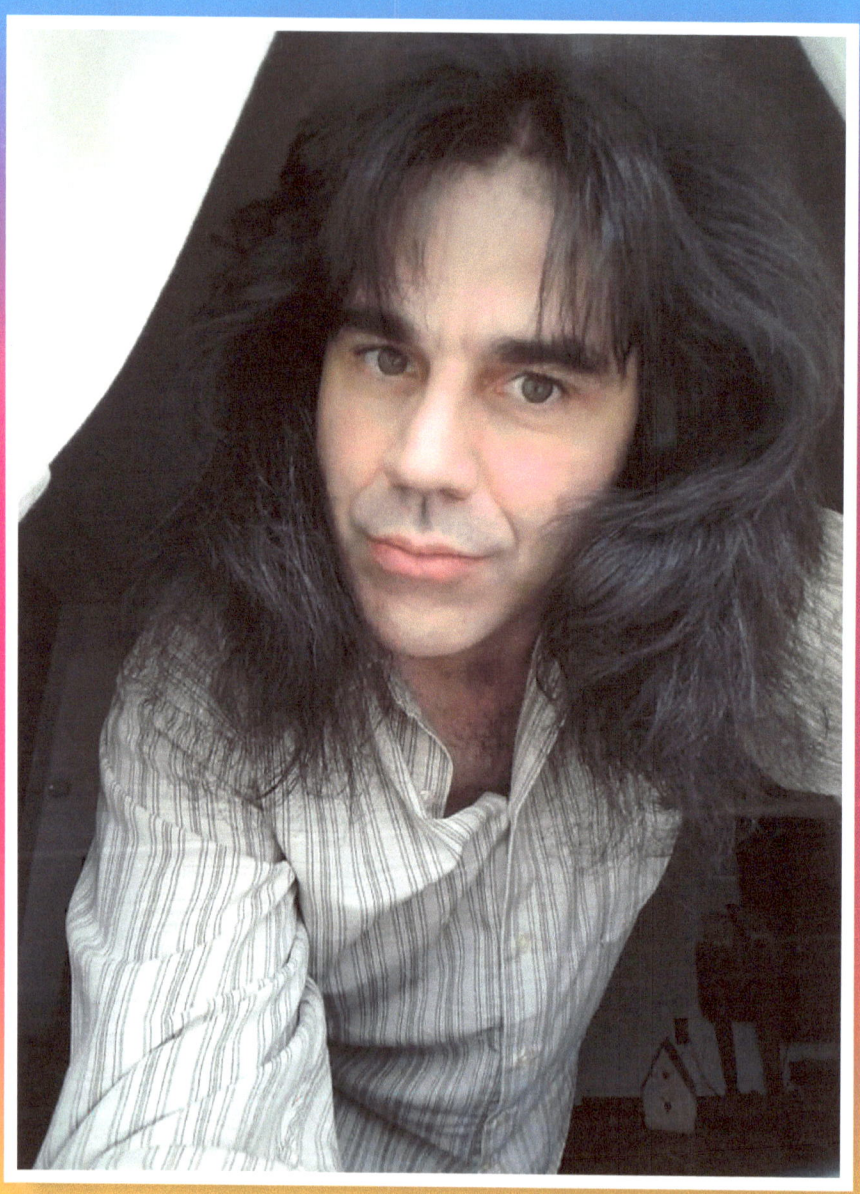

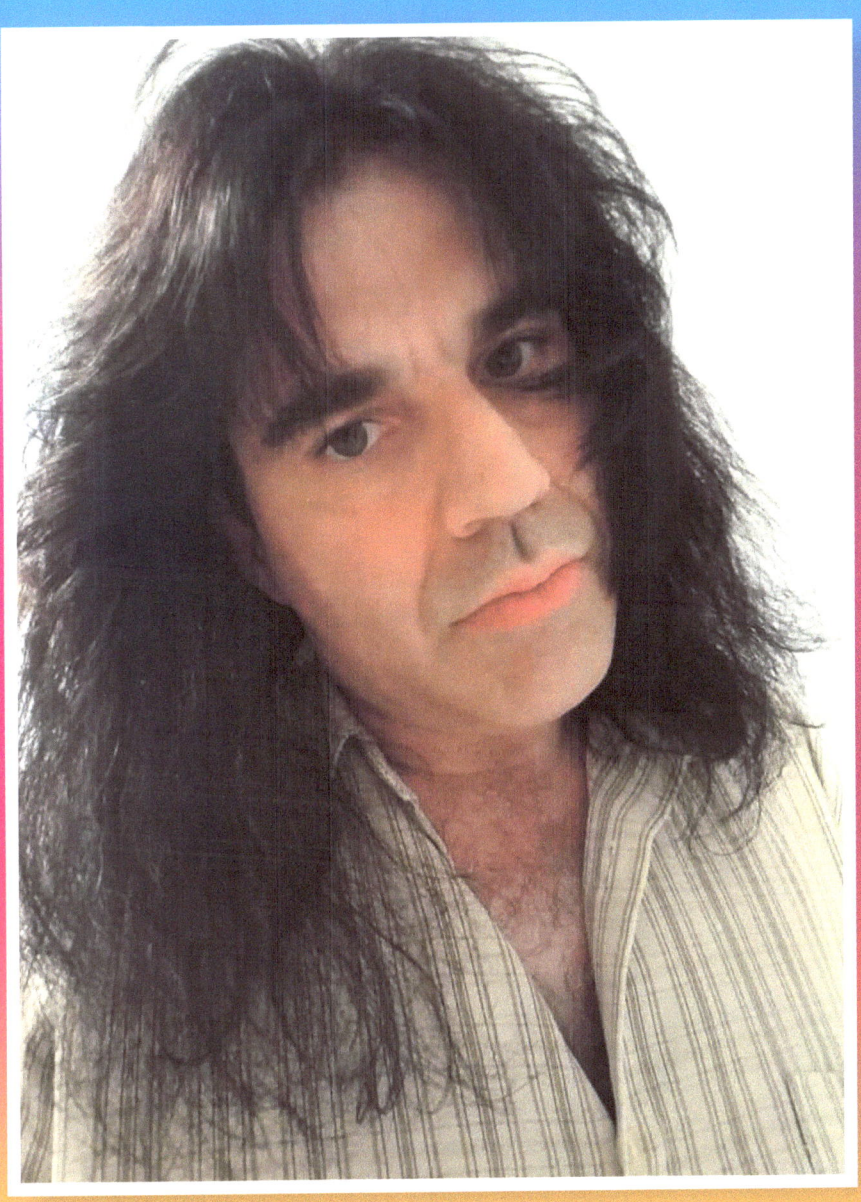

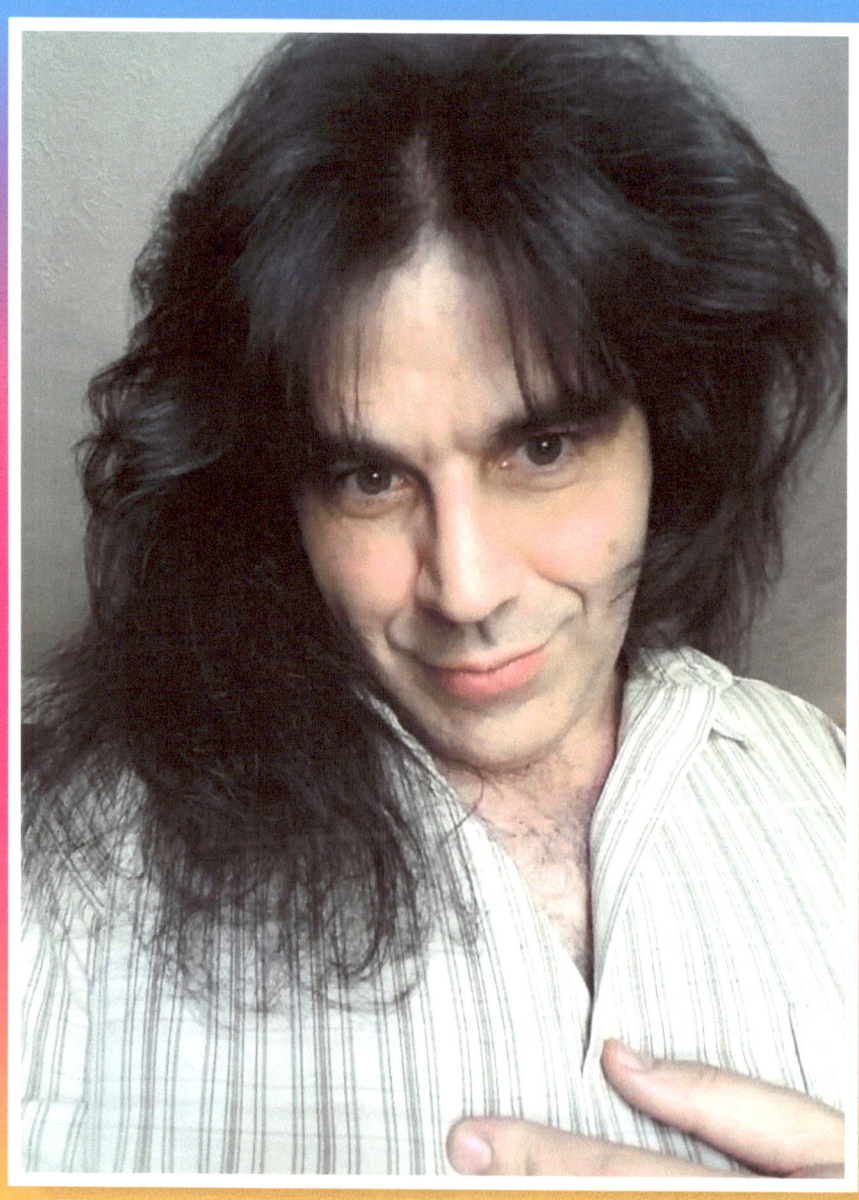

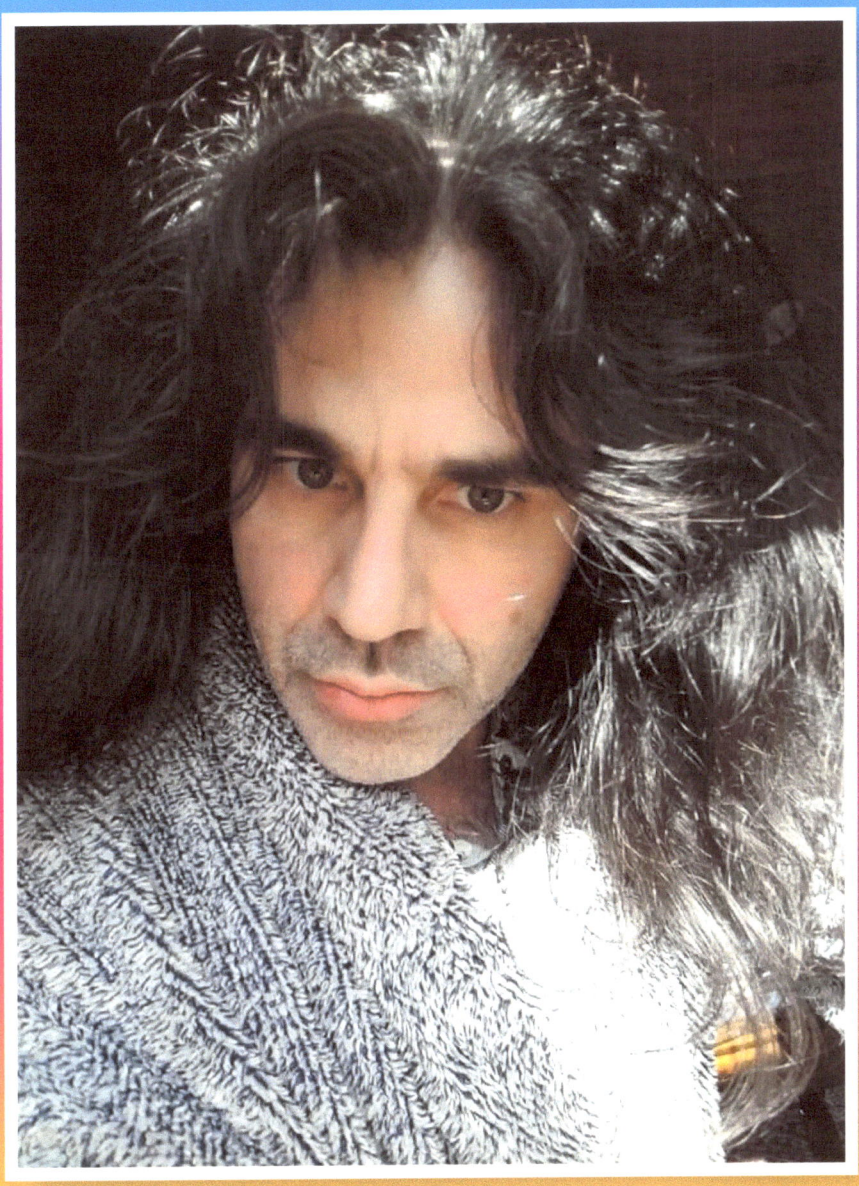